*quick reference to*

# PEDIATRIC
# CLINICAL
# SKILLS

# quick reference to
# PEDIATRIC CLINICAL SKILLS

**Ruth Bindler, RNC, MS**
Associate Professor
Intercollegiate Center for Nursing Education
Washington State University
Spokane, Washington

**Jane Ball, RN, CPNP, DrPH**
Director
Emergency Medical Services for Children National Resource Center
Children's National Medical Center
Washington, DC

Appleton & Lange
Stamford, Connecticut

www.appletonlange.com

99 00 01 02 03 / 10 9 8 7 6 5 4 3 2 1

Prentice Hall International (UK) Limited, *London*
Prentice Hall of Australia Pty. Limited, *Sydney*
Prentice Hall Canada, Inc., *Toronto*
Prentice Hall Hispanoamericana, S.A., *Mexico*
Prentice Hall of India Private Limited, *New Delhi*
Prentice Hall of Japan, Inc., *Tokyo*
Simon & Schuster Asia Pte. Ltd., *Singapore*
Editora Prentice Hall do Brasil Ltda., *Rio de Janeiro*
Prentice Hall, *Upper Saddle River, New Jersey*

ISBN: 0-8385-8123-4

Acquisitions Editor: David P. Carroll
Production Editors: Karen Davis, Angela Dion
Designers: Libby Schmitz, Aimee Nordin

PRINTED IN THE UNITED STATES OF AMERICA

ISBN 0-8385-8123-4

9 780838 1230  90000

# CONTENTS

## 12. IRRIGATION / 127

## APPENDICES / 131

# PREFACE

This *Quick Reference to Pediatric Clinical Skills* is designed to accompany the second edition of *Pediatric Nursing: Caring for Children*. An earlier version of this content was included as an atlas in the first edition of that book.

All of the skills content has been thoroughly updated, expanded, and reformatted, reflecting changes since the last edition. New skills have been added, new photographs provided to supplement existing skills, and new guidelines added for the use of protective equipment (gowns, masks, goggles, gloves). The format and organization of the *Quick Reference* continue to enable students to quickly learn and review what they need to do, when, and why. The *Quick Reference* has been bound and packaged separately from the text to enable students to carry it with them into clinical settings.

It is assumed that the student using this *Quick Reference* has had a course and practice in basic psychomotor skill performance. The information in this reference thus concentrates on pediatric variations of the most frequently used skills.

## ▶ ACKNOWLEDGMENTS

As with any published work, this *Quick Reference* is possible only because of the dedication and hard work of many people. Marcia Wellington provided the material for the first edition. Her contribution was thoughtful and provided guidance for those performing skills on children. Jane Novoa reviewed and provided important feedback for the first edition and George Dodson took all of the photographs.

The skills and procedures in this *Quick Reference* were carefully reviewed by Neysa Dobson for accuracy and currency. In addition, Karen Frank reviewed the original edition and provided feedback. Photos were taken by Roy Ramsey and content assistance during photography was provided by Neysa Dobson.

Throughout the entire process, Appleton & Lange editor David Carroll provided encouragement and support. His vision for this separate reference guide was instrumental in our taking this new approach. Our developmental editor, Donna Frassetto, has revised copy and suggested changes with a perceptive awareness of the needs of the reader and the presentation of material. Her role is an essential and creative one.

*Ruth Bindler*
*Jane Ball*

# INTRODUCTION

Children often undergo various procedures during diagnostic evaluation and hospitalization. These procedures, although similar to procedures performed on adults, differ in several ways. Nurses must therefore be knowledgeable about skills performed on children as well as variations in preparation, equipment, positioning, and specific steps when performing procedures on children.

Preparation for procedures must take into account a child's developmental stage and cognitive ability (see the discussion in Chapter 2 in the text of Ball and Bindler's *Pediatric Nursing*). General guidelines for preparing the child are outlined in the accompanying box. Follow these guidelines before beginning any procedure. After the procedure, provide emotional support and comfort the child.

Children should be taken either to a treatment room or to another room for potentially painful or frightening procedures. The child's room and the facility playroom are thus kept as "safe" areas in which painful procedures are not performed. It is best to have the parents present to support the child, either during or after the procedure. Other personnel can restrain the child. In this way, the child does not perceive the parents as participating in a hurtful activity.

Several steps should be taken when performing any procedure. These steps are listed in the accompanying box. Protective barriers such as clean or sterile gloves, gown, mask, and goggles should be worn during any procedure that may involve contact with blood or body fluids. Always check to see if the child has a latex allergy; if so, nonlatex gloves and equipment must be used.

The procedures in the *Quick Reference* are grouped into 12 units for ease of reference:

- Informed consent
- Positioning and restraint
- Transport
- Isolation precautions
- Physical assessment
- Specimen collection
- Administration of medication
- Intravenous access
- Cardiorespiratory care
- Nutrition
- Elimination
- Irrigation

Each procedure is presented concisely to emphasize essential information. Many procedures begin with brief lists of preparatory actions and equipment. These lists are not meant to be all-inclusive. Rather, they are

## GENERAL GUIDELINES

- Explain the procedure to the child and family.
- Ask if they have any questions about the procedure.
- If the parent agrees to hold the child, demonstrate exactly what you want done. Make sure that the parent feels comfortable about assisting with the procedure.
- Be familiar with the equipment.
- If the parent will not be present, reassure the child that the parent will return after the procedure has been completed.

## PROCEDURAL STEPS

1. Identify yourself to the child and parents.
2. Check the physician's orders.
3. Identify the child.
4. Give instructions and explanations to the child and parent.
5. Wash your hands.
6. Gather the necessary equipment.
7. Put on gloves.*
8. Begin the procedure.
9. Document findings.

*Gloves should be worn when it is possible that contact with mucous membranes, nonintact skin, or any body substances will occur. Gloves should be changed between different patient contacts.

intended to highlight equipment and information that is most important when performing the procedure on a child.

The procedures themselves are presented in a condensed format. It is understood that students have already learned the basic steps involved in these procedures. *The intent of this presentation is, therefore, to highlight essential steps and pediatric variations with which the nurse should be familiar.* Students should consult their hospital or institution procedure manual or other references for more detailed and specific information.

# INFORMED CONSENT 1

Informed consent involves obtaining written permission from the parent (or legal guardian) or the patient to perform specific procedures. Both legally and ethically necessary, informed consent requires that the parent or legal guardian and patient (to the level of the child's ability) clearly understand the procedure or treatment to be performed, any risk factors involved, and alternative methods available to achieve the same end. Without signed permission for medical management, the physician, nurse, or other health care provider could be found guilty of assault and battery.

## ► GENERAL GUIDELINES

Guidelines have been established to ensure that informed consent is obtained for medical care. Additional guidelines are available when performing research on children. These are not presented here.

- Information must be presented to the individual responsible for making an informed decision to allow him or her to weigh the benefits of the proposed treatment or procedure against the potential for complications. This information should be presented in simple, easy-to-understand terms. All questions and concerns should be answered honestly. If necessary, an interpreter should be used to ensure clear communication.

- The person making the decision must be over the age of majority (ie, the age at which full civil rights are accorded—18 years in most states) and must be competent (ie, he or she must be able to make a decision based on the information received). The person needs to understand the proposed medical management and any risks. In some states, adolescents between the ages of 13 and 18 years are able to sign for some treatment alone (ie, birth control, substance abuse treatment). Know the parameters of the state law where you practice nursing.
- The decision reached must be voluntary. The person making the decision must not be coerced, forced, or placed under duress while considering the options.

Although general written consent for care is obtained within the hospital setting during the admission process, specific consent must be obtained for procedures or treatments that include:

- Major surgery
- Minor surgery such as a cutdown, incision and drainage, closed reduction of a fracture, or fracture pinning
- Invasive diagnostic tests such as lumbar puncture, bone marrow aspiration, biopsy, cardiac catheterization, or endoscopy
- Treatments that may involve high risk, such as radiation therapy, chemotherapy, or dialysis
- Any procedure or treatment that falls under the auspices of research
- Photographing patients, even when done for educational purposes

## ► PEDIATRIC CONSIDERATIONS

Informed consent for the child involves the following additional considerations that must be addressed:

- *When the child is a minor* (has not reached the age of majority—under the age of 18 years in most states), his or her parent or legal guardian must give consent for all procedures or treatments.
- *If the parent or guardian is unavailable,* the person in charge of the child (eg, relative, baby-sitter, teacher, or camp counselor) may give consent for emergency treatment if the person has signed, written permission from the parent/guardian to authorize care in his or her absence.
- *If the parent or guardian can be contacted by telephone,* verbal consent can be obtained with two witnesses listening simultaneously. The consent should be recorded for later signature.
- *If the child is an emancipated minor* (under the age of 18 years but is legally independent), the child may give informed consent for medical care. Common examples of emancipated minors include teenagers who are married, in the military, living apart from their parents and financially independent, or parents themselves.
- *When the child is a minor living in a state providing the right for nonemancipated teens to make certain health care decisions,* the child may give permission only for those conditions identified in state law, and only at the ages specified by that particular state. Some examples of the treatments that many states permit adolescents to sign for include birth control, treatment of sexually transmitted diseases, contraceptive and abortion counseling and services, substance abuse, and mental illness.

# POSITIONING AND RESTRAINT 2

## ►UNIT OUTLINE

**HUMAN RESTRAINT**

*Restraining a child for intravenous
    access/injection*
*Restraining a child for lumbar
    puncture*

**MECHANICAL RESTRAINT**

Use of a Restraint Board
*Applying a restraint board*
Use of a Mummy Restraint
*Applying a mummy restraint*
Use of Elbow Restraints

### CLINICAL TIP

The American Academy of Pediatrics has established guidelines on the use of physical restraint for children and adolescents in the acute care setting. They recommend:

• Explaining the procedure to the child
• Obtaining a written or verbal order for restraint from the physician, stating the type of restraint and its expected duration
• Providing an immediate explanation to the family about the need for restraint and documenting this in the medical record
• Performing assessments: Is the restraint applied correctly? Are skin and neurovascular status intact? Is the restraint accomplishing its purpose? Is there a need to continue using restraint?

When a child must be held in position for a procedure, it is important to try to use an assistant rather than a mechanical restraint for this purpose. Though some parents are comfortable holding their child for a procedure, most prefer to be close and to act as a support person, while allowing health care professionals to provide restraint. This allows the parent to be free to provide support and to avoid the role of holding the child for a painful or stressful procedure. The child then can view the parent as a source of solace rather than as someone who brings pain. With the parent nearby, the child will be far less anxious and will not feel that he or she is being punished.

Some parents find it hard to be present during an uncomfortable procedure and prefer to be available afterward to comfort the child. This wish should be respected.

When necessary, a restraint board or mummy restraint can be used.

## ► HUMAN RESTRAINT

Be sure that the person providing restraint clearly understands what body parts must be held still and how to do this safely.

## RESTRAINING A CHILD FOR INTRAVENOUS ACCESS/INJECTION

### Procedure

- Place the child in a supine position on a bed or stretcher.
- Have the parent, a nurse, or an assistant lean over the child to restrain the child's body and extend the extremity to be used for access or injection.

## RESTRAINING A CHILD FOR LUMBAR PUNCTURE

### NURSING ALERT

Lumbar puncture requires that the child be held still. It is advisable to have an experienced staff member hold the child in position for the procedure.

### Procedure—*Gown, Goggles, Mask, Sterile Gloves*

- Place the child on his or her side with knees pulled to the abdomen and the neck flexed to the chin.
- The *infant* can be held in this position easily by holding the neck and thighs in your hands (Fig. 1).
- The *older child* can be quite strong, and someone with enough strength will be needed to hold him or her in this position. Lean over the child with your entire body, using your forearms against the thighs and around the shoulders and head.

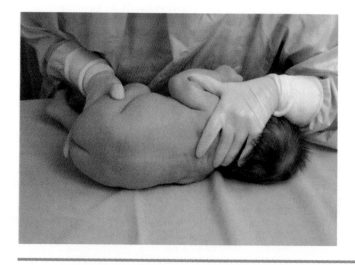

**FIGURE 1.** Infant positioned for lumbar puncture.

# ► MECHANICAL RESTRAINT

## USE OF A RESTRAINT BOARD

The restraint board consists of a board and cloth wrappings with Velcro fasteners (Fig. 2). Two sizes are available—one for infants and toddlers and one for larger children. Some restraint boards come with openings for arms. If the child is positioned for a venipuncture, the arm can fit through the opening in the vest and then the remaining fabric pieces can be secured.

### PROCEDURAL STEPS

1. Identify yourself to the child and parents.
2. Check the medical orders.
3. Identify the child.
4. Give instructions and explanation to the child and parent.
5. Wash your hands.
6. Gather the necessary equipment.
7. Use protective barriers as needed.
8. Begin the procedure.
9. Document findings.

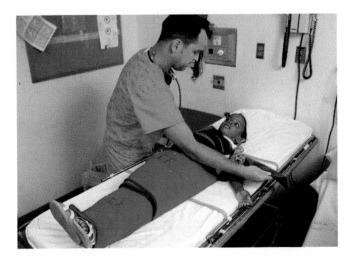

FIGURE 2. Child on a restraint board.

## APPLYING A RESTRAINT BOARD

### Preparation

Explain to the child and parents why the restraint is being used. Compare the feeling of the board to a hug.

### Selected Equipment

Board with fasteners
Soft towel or sheet

### Procedure

- Place a towel or sheet over the board.
- Have the child lie supine on the board, with the head at the top.
- Place the fabric wrappings around the child, and secure the Velcro fasteners.
- An assistant may be needed to provide restraint for the child's head and exposed extremity.

### GENERAL GUIDELINES

- Explain the procedure to the child and family.
- Ask if they have any questions about the procedure.
- If the parents decide to be present, demonstrate where they can stand and what they can do. Make sure that the parents feel comfortable about assisting with the procedure.
- Be familiar with the equipment.
- If the parents will not be present, reassure the child about when the parent will return.

## USE OF A MUMMY RESTRAINT

Mummy restraint consists of wrapping the child securely in a blanket or sheet to decrease movement and allow the health care provider to carry out a procedure. It is effective when procedures are being performed either on the head or on an extremity (one limb can be left out for the procedure).

## APPLYING A MUMMY RESTRAINT

### Preparation

- Use a blanket or sheet large enough to hold the child in place. Put the blanket (or sheet) on the bed or examination table.
- Explain to the child and parents why the restraint is being used.

### Selected Equipment

Soft blanket or sheet two to three times larger than the child

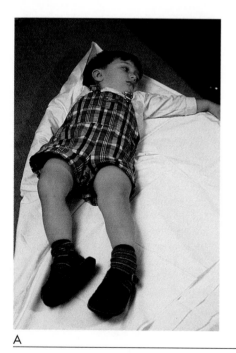
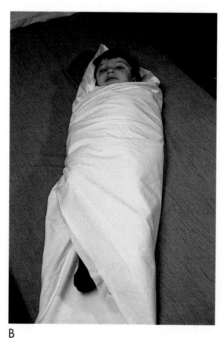
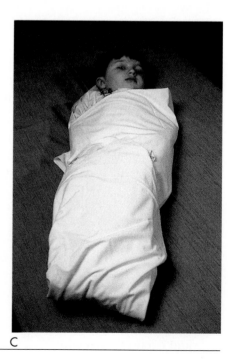

A    B    C

FIGURE 3. Steps in applying a mummy restraint.

## Procedure

### Infant, Toddler, and Older Child

- Place the child on the blanket, positioning so that there is sufficient material to wrap the knees and lower legs. If necessary, fold down the top edges of the blanket to the shoulders.
- Bring one side of the blanket up and tuck it under the arm on the same side, and place it under the child's back (Fig. 3A).
- Bring the other side of the blanket up and around the body, and tuck underneath the back and legs. (Fig. 3B).
- Bring the bottom corner of the blanket up and over the abdomen (Fig. 3C).

## USE OF ELBOW RESTRAINTS

Elbow restraints (Fig. 4) are used to prevent the infant or child from reaching his or her face or head. Although the ready-made type is available commercially, an elbow restraint can be devised easily from a piece of muslin that has vertical pockets sewn into it, as follows:

- Place tongue depressors in the vertical pockets of the muslin wrap so that the arm cannot be bent.
- Wrap the muslin around the arm from axilla to wrist.
- Secure the restraint with pins or tape.

Remove the elbow restraints at least every 2 hours to assess the child's skin and circulation.

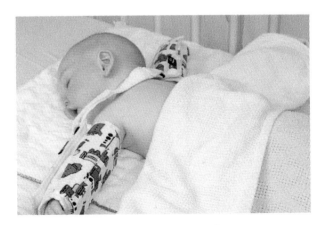

FIGURE 4. Infant with elbow restraints.

# TRANSPORT 3

► UNIT OUTLINE

TRANSPORT OF THE INFANT

TRANSPORT OF THE TODDLER

TRANSPORT OF THE CHILD WITH
A DISABILITY OR AN IMMOBILE
CHILD

 **HOME CARE CONSIDERATIONS**

When the child with medical equipment or casts is going to be discharged, assist the family to plan for car seats and alteration of the home to facilitate the child's needs. See Chapter 19 of Ball and Bindler's *Pediatric Nursing* for resources to offer parents.

Safety is the most important aspect of transporting infants and children. In determining the best method of transporting a child, the developmental stage must be taken into consideration. For safety, the child should be visible to the transporting adult at all times.

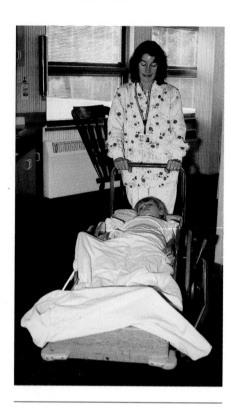

FIGURE 5. Technique for transporting an infant.

## ▶ TRANSPORT OF THE INFANT

The infant who is lying down, either on the side or supine, can be placed in a bassinet or crib for transport. If the bassinet has a bottom shelf, it can be used for carrying the IV pump or monitor. A wagon that can be pushed rather than pulled may also be used, and the IV pole can be pushed along with it (Fig. 5). The infant is kept covered with a blanket to avoid hypothermia resulting from a cool environment.

## ▶ TRANSPORT OF THE TODDLER

The toddler should be transported in a high-top crib (also used for infants, as shown in Fig. 6), with the siderails up and the protective top in place. The child may be sitting or lying down. Stretchers should not be used because the mobile toddler may roll or fall off.

A stroller or wheelchair may also be used, if available. Be sure to secure the child in the stroller with the seat safety strap. If a wheelchair is used, have the parent (if available) sit in the wheelchair and hold the toddler securely on his or her lap. Otherwise, a wheelchair that is the appropriate size for the child should be used.

FIGURE 6. High-top crib for infant or toddler transport.

## ► TRANSPORT OF THE CHILD WITH A DISABILITY OR AN IMMOBILE CHILD

For the older child who is unable to walk because of a disability or whose mobility must be restricted, a specially designed wagon (Fig. 7) can be used for transport. Close supervision is needed to ensure safety.

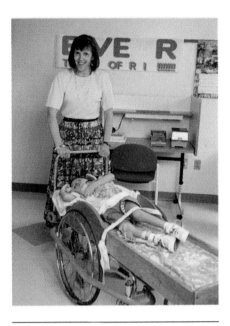

**FIGURE 7.** Technique for transporting a child with a disability.

# ISOLATION PRECAUTIONS 4

## ► ISOLATION EQUIPMENT

Isolation equipment consists of protective barriers (masks, gloves, gowns, and protective eyewear) that should be kept on a cart just outside the child's room for easy access (Fig. 8). Specific labels are available which explain each type of isolation and can be hung on the child's door.

### MASKS

Masks are used for protection from pathogens that are shed through respiratory droplets.

### GLOVES

Gloves are used to protect the skin from contact with pathogens. They protect the health care professional and the child from cross-contamination.

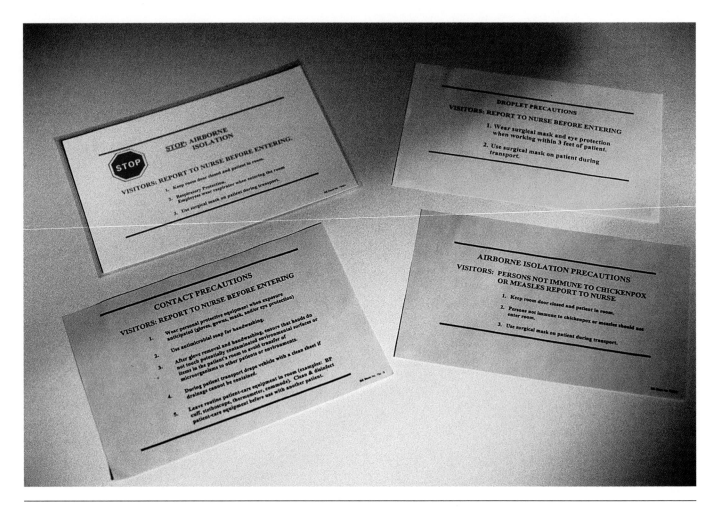

**FIGURE 8.** Isolation signs.

Gloves should be worn when it is likely that contact with mucous membranes, nonintact skin, or moist body substances will occur. They should be changed between contacts with different patients. Always use nonlatex gloves if the child has an allergy or sensitivity to latex, or if the health care provider has latex sensitivity (see Chapter 9 of Ball and Bindler's *Pediatric Nursing* for information on latex allergies).

## GOWNS

Gowns are used for protection against contact with pathogens. They should be worn when it is likely that body substances will come in contact with your clothing. Gowns should be changed between different patient contacts.

## PROTECTIVE EYEWEAR

Goggles or face shields should be worn if there is a risk of blood or body fluid being splattered. They should be worn (1) when there is a chance that your eye, nose, or mouth may be splashed with body substances or (2) when you are working in close proximity to any open skin lesions.

# ► ISOLATION METHODS

Isolation precautions are used to provide infection control. There are two levels of precautions: standard and transmission-based.

## STANDARD PRECAUTIONS

Standard precautions are used in the care of all patients, no matter what their diagnoses, whenever contact with blood, body fluids, secretions, excretions, nonintact skin, mucous membranes, or materials contaminated with these substances might occur. The following general guidelines should be used:

- Wash hands before and after patient contact and whenever needed during contact.
- Wear gloves whenever contact with blood, body fluids, secretions, excretions, nonintact skin, or mucous membranes might occur. Change gloves each time they are contaminated with these substances, washing hands before regloving.
- Wear additional protective equipment such as a gown, mask, and goggles if body fluid splashes may occur.
- Wear the protective equipment listed above to clean up body fluid spills. Discard waste in appropriate body substance waste containers. Clean the area with bleach or another acceptable cleaner. Bag contaminated laundry in secured and labeled bags.
- Discard needles, scalpels, and lancets in labeled sharps containers without recapping.

Patients who could contaminate the environment with airborne or droplet infection should be placed in private rooms.

## TRANSMISSION-BASED PRECAUTIONS

In addition to standard precautions, further measures are followed when a patient may be infected with a pathogen or communicable disease. There are three levels of precautions:

1. *Airborne.* Diseases transported by the airborne route (such as measles, chicken pox, and tuberculosis) require the use of high-efficiency particulate air filter respirators (or other respirators that filter inspired air) to protect care providers. For tuberculosis, a negative air flow ventilation system room is needed. The patient must wear a surgical mask when leaving the room to filter expired air. The room door is labeled with a sign instructing visitors to report to the nurses' station before entering.
2. *Droplet.* Diseases transmitted by the droplet route (such as *Haemophilus influenzae* type b, rubella, and pertussis) require the use of a surgical mask when coming within 3 feet of the patient. The patient wears a mask when leaving the room. The room door can remain open, and special respirators are not required since the large-particle droplets of these diseases cannot travel over 3 feet.

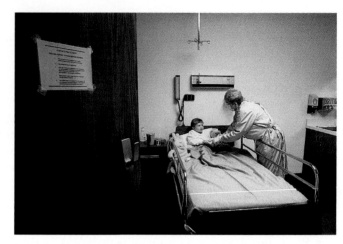

A

B

**FIGURE 9.** For patients in airborne isolation, gowns and masks may be worn **(A)**, and the door must be clearly labeled with a sign instructing visitors to stop at the nurse's station before entering **(B)**.

3. *Contact.* Diseases that are spread by direct contact with the skin or by indirect contact with a contaminated object in the patient's environment require the use of gloves during care. (Examples include most gastrointestinal and skin infections.) Gowns are worn if the health care professional's clothing may come in contact with contaminated surfaces or the patient (Fig. 9A). Patients should be placed in a private room or with other patients with the same pathogen (Fig. 9B).

# PHYSICAL ASSESSMENT 5

## ▶ UNIT OUTLINE

## ▶ GROWTH MEASUREMENTS

For a complete discussion of pediatric physical assessment, refer to Chapter 3 of Ball and Bindler's *Pediatric Nursing*. Physical growth charts for boys and girls are provided in Appendix A.

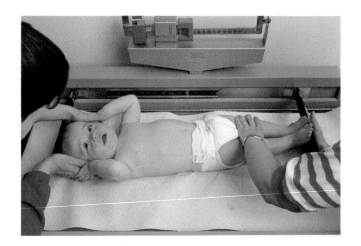

FIGURE 10. Measuring an infant's length.

## LENGTH

Until a child is 2 years of age, length is measured with the child in the supine position (Fig. 10). Because of the normally flexed posture of the infant, the body must be extended to obtain an accurate measurement. Hold the infant's head in the midline and gently push down on the knees until the legs are straight.

If a measuring board is used, place the infant's head against the top of the board and position the heels of the feet on the footboard. If such a device is not available, place the infant on a paper sheet. Make one mark at the vertex of the head and another at the heel. Then measure the distance between the two marks.

Record the length in centimeters or inches.

## HEIGHT

After the age of 2–3 years, height is measured with the child standing upright against a wall (Fig. 11). Have the child remove his or her shoes and stand straight with the head erect and in the midline position. The shoulders, buttocks, and heels should touch the wall. Place a flat surface such as a ruler on top of the child's head. Make a mark where the ruler's edge hits the wall. Measure the distance from the mark to the floor. An object called a stadiometer can be permanently attached to the wall for greater accuracy. It has a movable top that is placed on the child's head; a reading of height is then made on the stadiometer (see Fig. 11). In the older child, height is measured using a platform scale with an attached stature-measuring device.

Record the height in centimeters or inches.

FIGURE 11. Measuring a child's height.

## WEIGHT

Infants are weighed on a platform scale (Fig. 12), either in a supine or sitting position, depending on their age. Check the balance of the scale before placing the infant on it, and put a paper cover on the scale. Care should be taken to ensure the infant's safety. Infants should be weighed without clothing or diapers. Remember to change the paper covering after weighing.

The older child's weight can be measured on a standing scale. Toddlers should be weighed in their underclothes. Older children can remain in their street clothes with sweaters and shoes removed. Keep the room warm for comfort and provide privacy for the older child and adolescent.

Record the weight in kilograms or pounds.

## HEAD CIRCUMFERENCE

Head circumference is usually measured at regular intervals until the child's first or second birthday. Measure the head at its greatest circumference, just above the brow, just above the pinna of the ears, and around the occipital prominence (Fig. 13). Use a paper tape measure, and record the circumference in inches or centimeters.

## CHEST CIRCUMFERENCE

Chest circumference is often measured until 1 year of age. Measure the chest with a tape measure placed just under the axilla, over the nipple line (Fig. 14).

Record the circumference in centimeters or inches. Compare chest circumference to head circumference measurement. They will be approximately equal until after one year of age, when chest circumference begins to surpass head circumference.

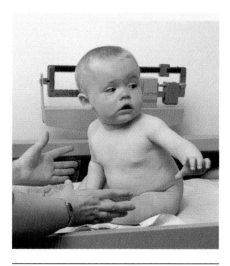

FIGURE 12. A platform scale is used to weigh an infant.

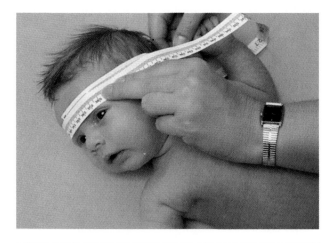

FIGURE 13. Measuring head circumference.

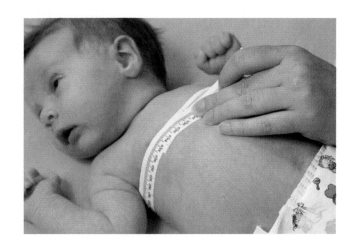

FIGURE 14. Measuring chest circumference.

## ▶ VITAL SIGNS

Assessment of vital signs is also discussed in Chapter 3 of Ball and Bindler's *Pediatric Nursing.*

### HEART RATE

The apical heart rate is preferred in children. To count the rate, place the stethoscope on the anterior chest at the fifth intercostal space in a midclavicular position. Each "lub-dub" sound is one beat. Count the beats for 1 full minute. While auscultating the heart rate, note whether the rhythm is regular or irregular.

Pulse rates may be checked at sites other than the apex, for example, the carotid, brachial, radial, femoral, and dorsal pedis sites. Compare the distal and proximal pulses for strength. Compare the upper and lower pulses for strength. Also record whether the pulse is normal, bounding (very strong), or thready (weak).

The range of normal heart rates based on age is listed in Table 1.

| 1 | Range of Normal Heart Rates in Children, Birth to 14 Years | |
|---|---|---|
| **Age** | | **Range (beats/min)** |
| Newborn | | 100–170 |
| 6 mo–1 yr | | 90–130 |
| 3 yr | | 80–120 |
| 5 yr | | 70–110 |
| 10–14 yr | | 60–100 |

### RESPIRATORY RATE

The procedure for measuring a child's respiratory rate is essentially the same as for an adult. However, keep in mind these points:

- Since a child's respirations are diaphragmatic, observe abdominal movement to count respirations.
- Abdominal movement in a child will be irregular.

The range of normal respiratory rates based on age is listed in Table 2. Count breaths for 1 full minute.

| 2 | Range of Normal Respiratory Rates in Children, Birth to 17 Years | |
|---|---|---|
| | Age | Range (breaths/min) |
| | Newborn | 30–80 |
| | 6 mo | 24–36 |
| | 1 yr | 20–40 |
| | 3 yr | 20–30 |
| | 6 yr | 16–22 |
| | 10 yr | 16–20 |
| | 17 yr | 12–20 |

## BLOOD PRESSURE

Blood pressure measurement for the child is basically the same as for an adult. Whether manual or electronic equipment is being used, the size of the blood pressure cuff is determined by the size of the child's arm or leg. Generally, the width of the bladder cuff is two thirds of the length of the long bone of the extremity on which the blood pressure is taken. The length of the bladder should be about three-fourths the circumference of the extremity and should not overlap (Fig. 15). If the bladder is too small, the pressure will be falsely high; if it is too large, the pressure will be falsely low.

FIGURE 15. Blood pressure cuffs are available in various types and sizes for pediatric patients.

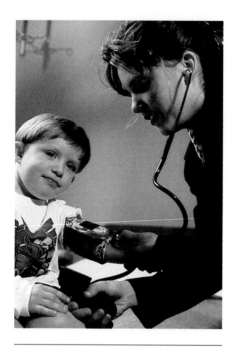

FIGURE 16. Measuring blood pressure with a manual cuff.

If electronic equipment is being used, place the cuff around the desired extremity and activate the equipment according to the manufacturer's recommendations.

If a manual cuff is being used, wrap the cuff around the desired extremity. Close the air escape valve. Palpate for the pulse, and place the stethoscope over the pulse area (Fig. 16). Pump the cuff with the bulb until the mercury rises and no beat is auscultated; continue pumping until the mercury rises another 20–30 mm. Slowly release the air through the valve at 2–3 mm/sec while watching the falling column of mercury. Note the number at which the first return of a pulse is heard; this is the systolic pressure. Continue releasing the air to determine the diastolic pressure: If the child is younger than 12 years, a muffled sound will be heard and is recorded at the diastolic pressure; if the child is older than 12 years, all sound will disappear at the diastolic pressure. Blood pressure is read as systolic over diastolic pressure (Table 3).

| 3 | Median Systolic and Diastolic Blood Pressure Values for Children of Different Ages[a] | |
| --- | --- | --- |
| Age | Systolic (mm Hg) | Diastolic (mm Hg) |
| Newborn | 73 | 55 |
| 1 mo | 86 | 52 |
| 6 mo | 90 | 53 |
| 1 yr | 90 | 56 |
| 3 yr | 92 | 55 |
| 6 yr | 96 | 57 |
| 9 yr | 100 | 61 |
| 12 yr | 107 | 64 |
| 15 yr | 114 | 65 |
| 18 yr | 121 | 70 |

[a]Readings show 50th percentile.
**Note:** Children who are in the 95th percentile for blood pressure for their age, gender, and height should be referred for hypertensive workup. See the following references for these standards: Joint National Committee on Prevention, Detection, Evaluation and Treatment of High Blood Pressure and the National High Blood Pressure Education Program Coordinating Committee. (1997). The sixth report of the Joint National Committee on Prevention, Detection, Evaluation, and Treatment of High Blood Pressure. *Archives of Internal Medicine, 157,* 2413–2443; and National High Blood Pressure Program Working Group on Hypertension Control in Children and Adolescents. (1996). Update on the 1987 task force report on high blood pressure in children and adolescents: A working group report from the National High Blood Pressure Education Program. *Pediatrics, 98*(4), 649–658.
*Adapted from the Normal Blood Pressure Readings for Boys from the Second Task Force on Blood Pressure Control in Children, National Heart, Lung, and Blood Institute (1987), Bethesda, MD. Normal blood pressure readings for girls are very similar to those for boys at all age groups.*

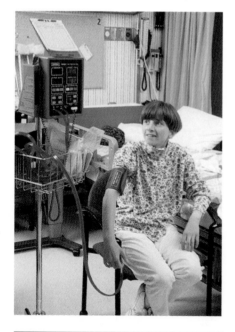

FIGURE 17. Measuring blood pressure using Doppler ultrasonography.

If the pulse cannot be auscultated, blood pressure can still be measured by touch. Wrap the cuff around the desired extremity, close the air valve, and palpate for the pulse. Keeping your fingers on the pulse, pump the cuff with the bulb until the pulse is no longer felt. Slowly open the air valve, watching the column of mercury, and note the number at which the pulse is again palpated. This is the palpated systolic blood pressure read as the number over "P."

Systolic pressure can also be measured by using Doppler ultrasonography (Fig. 17). With this technique, the frequency of ultrasonic waves is reflected by movement of the surface of the blood vessels, which differs slightly from that of other structures in the same area. Pressure is recorded as the number over "D."

# BODY TEMPERATURE

Body temperature can be measured on two scales: Fahrenheit or centigrade. If an electronic thermometer is being used, follow the manufacturer's guidelines. There is no documented "universal" agreement on the length of time that a mercury thermometer should be kept in place. Follow the guidelines of your hospital or institution. General recommendations usually list 3–5 minutes for oral, 2–5 minutes for rectal, and 6–8 minutes for axillary.

The four routes for measuring body temperature are tympanic, oral, rectal, and axillary.

## Tympanic Route

The tympanic route (Fig. 18) is a convenient and fast method for taking temperatures in infants and children.

Make sure the thermometer tip is aimed toward the tympanic membrane to ensure accuracy. Always use a clean probe tip for each child.

If you are using the child's right ear, hold the thermometer in your right hand. For the child's left ear, hold the thermometer in your left hand.

**HOME AND COMMUNITY CARE CONSIDERATIONS**

Ask parents what type of thermometer they use at home and provide instruction in its correct use. Often parents do not know how to shake down a mercury thermometer, resulting in faulty readings. They may not know for how long to insert the thermometer or how to clean and store it after use. Nurses in schools and day-care centers should assess the knowledge of the care providers in these settings and provide teaching as needed.

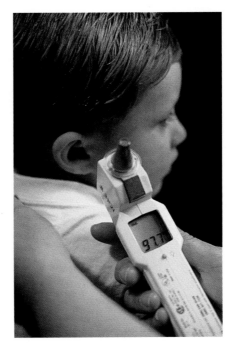

A                    B

FIGURE 18. **A,** Position for inserting thermometer when tympanic route is used. **B,** Digital readout of temperature appears within 1 minute.

## ASSESSING BODY TEMPERATURE USING THE TYMPANIC ROUTE

### Selected Equipment

Thermometer (electronic)

### Procedure

#### Child Younger Than 1 Year

- Place the infant in a supine position on a flat surface.
- Stabilize the infant's head.
- Turn the infant's head 90 degrees for easy access.
- Pull the pinna of the ear straight back and downward.
- Approach the ear from behind to direct the tip of the probe anteriorly.
- Place the probe in the ear as far as possible to seal the canal.
- Turn on the scanner.
- Leave the probe in the ear according to the manufacturer's recommendations.
- Remove the probe.
- Read and record the temperature.

#### Child Older Than 1 Year

- Have the parent hold the child on his or her lap, keeping the child's head against his or her chest for support. The child's arms and legs may need to be held.
- Pull the pinna back and up in children over about 3 years or back and downward under that age.
- Place the probe and continue as described above for the child younger than 1 year.
- Read and record the temperature.

## Oral Route

The oral route may be used for the child over 3 years of age. (An electronic nonbreakable probe is preferred.)

 **ASSESSING BODY TEMPERATURE USING THE ORAL ROUTE**

### Selected Equipment

Thermometer (glass with oral bulb—usually blue tipped) or electronic thermometer with sheath

### Procedure—*Clean Gloves*

- Place the oral probe or an electronic thermometer (with protective sheath) or the glass thermometer under the tongue and have the child close his or her mouth.
- If electronic equipment is being used, turn on the scanner and follow the manufacturer's recommendations. It will sound a tone or beep when finished. Remove the probe.
- If you are using a glass thermometer, keep it in place for approximately 3–5 minutes; then read the temperature based on the column of mercury.
- Read and record the temperature.

### Rectal Route

The rectal route should be used only when no other route is possible. It is not recommended because of the potential for rectal perforation and because most children view this as an intrusive procedure. The rectal temperature is one degree higher than the oral temperature.

## ASSESSING BODY TEMPERATURE USING THE RECTAL ROUTE

### Selected Equipment

Thermometer (electronic or rectal—with stubby bulb and usually red tipped) or electronic thermometer with sheath
Protective sheath for glass thermometer
Water-soluble lubricant

### Procedure—*Clean Gloves*

- Place the infant or child prone on a bed or the parent's lap; turn the older child on the side.
- Cover the tip of the rectal probe of an electronic thermometer (with protective sheath) or the glass thermometer (with protective sheath) with a water-soluble lubricant.
- For the infant, place the tip ¼ to ½ inch into the rectum.
- For the child, place the tip 1 inch into the rectum.
- If electronic equipment is being used, turn on the scanner and follow the manufacturer's recommendations. It will sound a tone or beep when finished. Remove the probe.
- If you are using a glass thermometer, hold the thermometer in place for 2–5 minutes.
- Read and record the temperature.

## Axillary Route

The axillary route (Fig. 19) is often used for children who are seizure-prone, unconscious, or immunosuppressed, or who have a structural abnormality that precludes an alternate route. It may be used in settings such as schools where the least invasive route is desired. The axillary temperature is one degree lower than the oral temperature. Current research indicates that this method is not as accurate as other methods in identifying children with fevers.

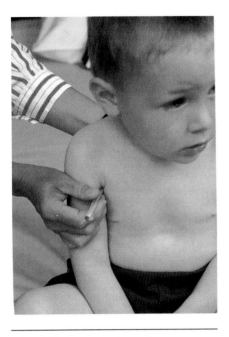

**FIGURE 19.** Measuring the axillary temperature.

## ASSESSING BODY TEMPERATURE USING THE AXILLARY ROUTE

### Selected Equipment

Thermometer (glass with any bulb) or electronic thermometer with sheath

### Procedure

- The probe with sheath (on electronic model) or the thermometer (rectal or oral) is held in place in the axilla, with the child's arm pressed close to his or her side.
- If you are using an electronic probe, wait for the tone before removing it to read the temperature. If you are using a glass thermometer, keep it in place for approximately 6–8 minutes before reading it.
- Read and record the temperature.

## ► OXYGEN SATURATION: PULSE OXIMETRY

Pulse oximetry is a simple noninvasive means of measuring the oxygen saturation of the blood ($SaO_2$).

## USING A PULSE OXIMETER

### Preparation

Emphasize that pulse oximetry is a pain-free procedure.

### Selected Equipment

Pulse oximeter
Appropriate-size sensor

### Procedure

- Assess the child's condition before attaching the sensor. Check respiratory status, including heart rate, respiratory rate, skin color, and respiratory effort.
- The sensor may be placed on the fingertip over the nail (Fig. 20), on the toe over the nail, or on the ear lobe (if the child is cold or has poor perfusion). It should be approximately at heart level.
- Probes come in two sizes: infant and pediatric. Size is determined by the size of the child and/or the placement site.
- Turn on the oximeter. Set parameters for alarms according to physician's orders. Attach the sensor to the machine. Watch for readout of pulse rate and oxygen saturation.
- You may leave the oximeter on for continuous readouts.

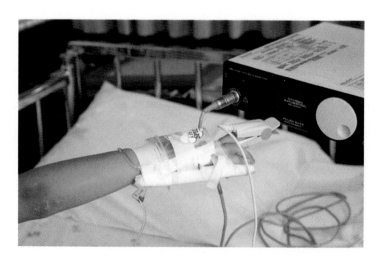

FIGURE 20. Pulse oximetry measurement.

- If frequent, but not continuous, monitoring is indicated, leave the sensor on the child but disconnect it from the machine.
- If the sensor is removed, place it on the plastic backing for further use.
- Always remove the sensor from the extremity at least every 2 hours to check the condition of the skin.

## ► CARDIORESPIRATORY MONITORING EQUIPMENT

The standard cardiorespiratory monitor measures heart rate and respiratory rate. The high and low limits are set according to the age of the child. Usually a 15–20-second period of apnea will set off the alarm.

An apnea monitor (Fig. 21) is used to monitor for abnormal or irregular breathing.

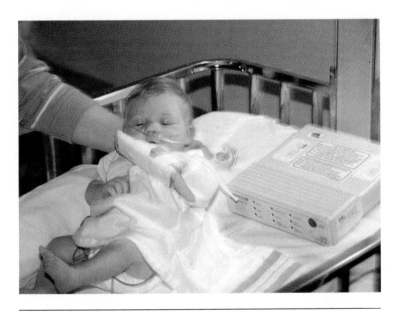

FIGURE 21. Apnea monitor.

## USING A CARDIORESPIRATORY MONITOR

### Selected Equipment

Cardiorespiratory monitor
Electrodes and straps to hold them in place
Alcohol swabs

### Procedure

- Clean the skin areas where the leads will be applied with alcohol swabs and allow to dry.
- Place leads on the infant's or child's chest: one on the right side, one on the left, and one (ground) on the lateral side of the abdomen (Fig. 22).

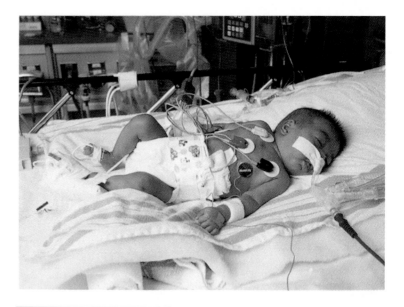

FIGURE 22. Placement of leads in cardiorespiratory monitoring.

- If the monitor sounds, check the child immediately. Assess breathing and heart rate.
- If the child is not in distress, silence the alarm, check the connections and leads, and reset the alarm.
- If the child is not breathing, stimulate the child and, if there is no response, initiate cardiopulmonary resuscitation (CPR). (CPR procedures are described in Unit 9.)

# ► VISUAL ACUITY

Several procedures may be used to screen visual acuity in children. Follow instructions carefully for the screening method you use. A few common methods are explained here.

## SNELLEN LETTER CHART

The Snellen letter (alphabet) chart (Fig. 23A) is the most commonly used assessment tool for visual acuity. It consists of lines of letters in decreasing size. Most often a chart designed to be read from a distance of 20 feet is used. If the child reads the line designated "20 feet" when standing 20 feet away, vision is "20/20." If however, the child can only read the line labeled "40 feet" while standing 20 feet away, vision is "20/40." Charts are also available that can be used at a distance of 10 feet (Fig 23B). A child who stands 10 feet from this chart and reads the 10-foot line (10/10) has vision equivalent to that of 20/20 when using the 20-foot chart.

## SNELLEN E CHART

For toddlers and children who have not yet mastered the alphabet, the Snellen E chart (Fig. 23C) or picture chart may be used. In the E chart the capital letter E is shown facing in different directions. The child is asked to point in the direction of the "legs" of the E. Another option is to give the child a paper with an E on it and have the child turn it in the direction the E is pointing on the chart. A variation of this test is the Blackbird Eye Test in which a blackbird flies in a shape similar to an E. The child identifies which direction the bird is flying.

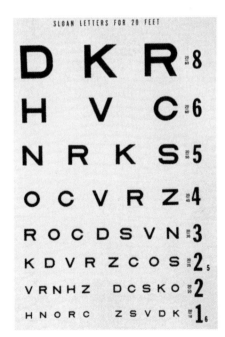

A

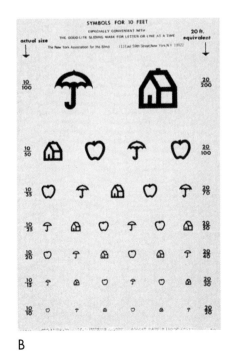

B

C

**FIGURE 23.** Visual acuity charts. **A,** Snellen letter chart. **B,** Picture chart. **C,** Snellen E chart.
*A and B, Courtesy of the National Society to Prevent Blindness, Schaumberg, IL.*

## PICTURE CHART

The picture chart (Fig. 23B) shows commonly identified silhouettes (eg, house, apple, umbrella) lined up. The child is asked to identify the picture.

## HOTV

For the HOTV eye test, the child looks at an HOTV chart positioned either 10 or 20 feet away and either names the letters or points to them on a card held close by. The procedure followed is the same as with the Snellen test, but because children can point to the letters on the chart in front of them, they do not need to know the alphabet. The HOTV test can also be used after a practice session with children who do not speak English. (HOTV does not represent words. These are the letters chosen to use in this eye test due to their differences in structure.)

## ASSESSING VISUAL ACUITY

### Procedure

- With the toddler, make a game of identifying the direction of the E or the picture.
- Place the heels of the child at the 20-foot mark (or 10-foot mark if using that type of chart).
- Be sure the chart is at the child's eye level and well lit.
- Assess each eye separately and then both together.
- While one eye is being tested, use a small piece of clean paper or eye occluder (cleaned after each child's use) to cover the other eye. Tell the child to keep the covered eye open during the testing. If the child wears glasses, check the vision both with and without glasses. If the child is wearing contact lenses, leave them in and note that the results were with contact lenses.
- Observe for squinting, moving the head forward (to be closer to the chart), excessive blinking, or tearing during the examination.
- Record the last line the child can read correctly (ie, the last line in which the child reads more than half the symbols on the line). Passing standards for visual acuity testing based on age are as follows:
  *3–5 years:* 20/40
  *Above 5 years:* 20/30

*Note:* Though these are passing standards, most children achieve 20/20 vision by 6 years of age. See Chapter 3, page 115, of *Pediatric Nursing* for expected visual acuity at various ages. Most states have laws regulating the ages or grades at which children must be screened and what passing standards are accepted. Check your state laws or codes for guidelines.

## REFERRALS

When a child's vision is not within the passing standards range for his or her age, the child should be rescreened in 1–2 weeks. If the results are still unsatisfactory, make the appropriate referral to the child's pediatrician or other health care provider, an ophthalmologist, or an optometrist.

## ► FLUID AND ELECTROLYTE BALANCE: INTAKE AND OUTPUT

Intake and output (I and O) is a measurement of fluid and electrolyte balance in the body.

Input is a measurement of what is delivered to the child through parenteral or oral routes. It is recorded in cubic centimeters (cc) or milliliters (mL). Output is a measurement of what is expelled, drained, secreted, or suctioned from the body. Output sources include urine, stool, vomitus, sweat, drainage from wounds, and nasogastric suction. Output can be measured easily in a graduated cylinder and is recorded in cubic centimeters (cc) or milliliters (mL).

Accurate measurement of I and O needs to be documented if the child is receiving IV fluids, has had major surgery, suffers from renal disease or kidney damage, is oliguric, is in congestive heart failure, has diabetes mellitus, is dehydrated, is hypovolemic, has suffered severe thermal burns, is taking medications such as diuretics or corticosteroids, or has a head injury, meningitis, or signs of increased intracranial pressure.

Clean gloves are worn whenever output measurements are done. Other protective barriers such as gowns should be worn if body fluids might splash onto your clothing. See Unit 4 on isolation precautions for further clarification.

## INFANT

For the infant, there are two methods of measuring urine or stool output:

1. Diapers can be weighed dry and then again after the infant has voided or stooled. For each 1-gram increase in weight of the diaper, 1 mL of liquid has been excreted by the infant. Disadvantages of this system include the inability to differentiate between urine and stool weights since the two substances may mix in the diaper, and the evaporation of urine that takes place after about 30 minutes. Counting the number of wet diapers is also used, since the amount of micturation is fairly standard during infancy and early toddlerhood. Four to eight wet diapers per day is usually normal.
2. A urine bag (see the discussion of specimen collection in Unit 6) may be used to obtain a more accurate measurement. Watch for any leakage.

## TODDLER AND OLDER CHILD

For the toddler and older child, urine and stool output can be measured in a bedpan. Pour the bedpan contents into a graduated cylinder for measurement. When the child is using the bathroom, a collection device can be placed over the toilet bowl but under the seat to collect output. (See Fig. 25, p. 40.) Instruct the child or parents to inform you when the child voids or stools so the output can be measured.

# SPECIMEN COLLECTION 6

In the collection of any type of specimen, it is the nurse's responsibility to be sure that the specimen is collected accurately, labeled correctly, and sent to the laboratory using any special techniques needed, such as immediate transport or maintenance on ice.

## ▶ BLOOD SAMPLES

There are two methods of obtaining blood samples in children: venipuncture and capillary puncture. For both methods the following preparation is necessary:

- Prepare the child and parents emotionally for the procedure.
- Have another nurse, an assistant, or the parent ready to restrain the child.

Communication strategies for a toddler undergoing venipuncture are presented in Table 4–9 of Ball and Bindler's *Pediatric Nursing*.

## VENIPUNCTURE

Venipuncture, or the puncturing of a vein, is used to obtain a sample for complete blood count, blood culture, sedimentation rate, blood type and crossmatch, blood clotting times, drug screen, ammonia level, fibrinogen level, and other tests.

## PERFORMING A VENIPUNCTURE

### Preparation

Choose the appropriate site. The veins of the antecubital fossa or forearm are usually the best choice because of their accessibility. However, the dorsum of the hand or foot also may be used. (Refer to pp. 64–65 of Unit 8.)

### Selected Equipment

Tourniquet
20–27-gauge needle with attached syringe (slightly larger than volume of blood needed)
Large-bore (19-gauge) needle
Appropriate blood collection tubes

## Procedure—*Clean Gloves*

- Place a tourniquet proximal to the desired vein to distend it. If necessary, hold the extremity below heart level, gently rub or tap the vein, or apply a warm compress to promote dilation of the vein.
- Locate the vein by inspection (wiping with alcohol will make the vein shine) or palpation.
- Once the vein has been located, clean the skin with alcohol or povidone–iodine, using an outward circular motion. Let dry.
- With your nondominant hand, hold the skin taut, gently pulling with your thumb just under the site of the puncture.
- Puncture the skin with the needle, bevel up at a 15-degree angle and directed toward the vein. When blood appears in the tube, gently pull back on the syringe.
- Release the tourniquet after all the blood has been collected. Remove the needle at the same angle used for entry and apply pressure to the site with gauze (alcohol will sting).
- Have the assistant or parent maintain pressure for a few minutes until the bleeding has stopped, at which point an adhesive bandage can be placed. Meanwhile, remove the butterfly needle from the syringe.
- Attach the large-bore (19-gauge) needle, and expel blood into the appropriate collection tubes as soon as possible.

 **CLINICAL TIP**

- Make sure the tourniquet is tight enough to restrict venous (but not arterial) blood flow.
- Keep the bevel of the needle up. Do not draw back too hard on the syringe because the vein will collapse.
- If blood fails to enter the tubing, the needle may not be placed correctly in the vein. Advance the needle slightly.
- If a flash was seen but blood no longer appears, the needle may be located incorrectly in the vein. Gently draw back on the needle.

# CAPILLARY PUNCTURE

A capillary puncture may be used to obtain a sample for complete blood count, reticulocyte count, platelet count, or blood chemistries such as electrolyte, glucose, or drug levels.

## PERFORMING A CAPILLARY PUNCTURE

### Preparation

Choose the appropriate site. Puncture sites include the plantar surface of the heel (Fig. 24) (for newborns and children under the age of 1 year), the great toe (for children over 1 year), and the palmar surface of the tip of the third or fourth finger.

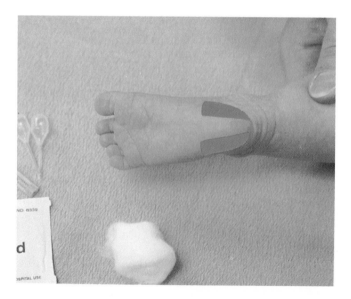

FIGURE 24. Heel sites for capillary puncture.

## Selected Equipment

Alcohol swabs
Lancet
Appropriate micro-size blood collection tubes

## Procedure—*Clean Gloves*

- Isolate the site to be used for capillary puncture.
  - *Finger stick.* Hold the child's hand with your nondominant hand (or have an assistant hold it), keeping the finger to be used extended and pointed down.
  - *Heel stick.* Hold the child's foot in your nondominant hand, supporting the dorsum of the foot with your thumb and the ankle with your other fingers.
  - *Toe stick.* Grasp the child's foot across the dorsum with your nondominant hand, supporting the toe with your thumb on the plantar surface.
- Clean the site with alcohol.
- Using your dominant hand, pierce the skin with the lancet.
- Wipe the first drop of blood away with the gauze.
- Using a milking motion, gently squeeze the site and direct the blood into the appropriate tube.
- When collection is complete, have an assistant hold the gauze on the site until the bleeding has stopped. Apply an adhesive bandage.

## ► URINE SAMPLES

A urine sample is obtained to assess for output amount, infection, and to determine levels of blood, protein, glucose, acetone, bilirubin, drugs, hormones, metals, and electrolytes. Urine can also be evaluated for concentration/specific gravity, pH, and crystals or other substances. Urine samples may need to be collected in a sterile or nonsterile manner. Simple collection devices are available for nonsterile collection (Fig. 25).

**FIGURE 25.** A urine collection device for the toilet.

## CLEAN-CATCH COLLECTION

A collection bag is used to obtain a urine sample from an infant or child who is not yet toilet trained. The bags come in two sizes: newborn and pediatric.

After being given clear instructions, older children are usually capable of collecting their own urine. Younger children will need assistance from the nurse, an assistant, or their parents.

## APPLYING A URINE COLLECTION BAG (INFANT)

### Selected Equipment

Urine collection bag
Soap solution, sterile water, and sterile cotton balls or packaged cleansing swabs for cleaning genitalia
Urine specimen container

### Procedure—*Clean Gloves*

#### *To Place the Bag Correctly*

- Remove the diaper and clean the skin around the meatus. Remove gloves, wash hands, and apply new gloves. Wipe the genital area with a cotton ball and soap about three times (from the tip of the penis toward the scrotum for boys, and the clitoris toward the anus for girls). Repeat using sterile water and cotton balls to rinse. Use each cotton ball only once and discard. Alternately, about three packaged wipes can be used as described.
- Attach the bag with the adhesive tabs (Fig. 26): for girls, around the labia; for boys, around the scrotum.

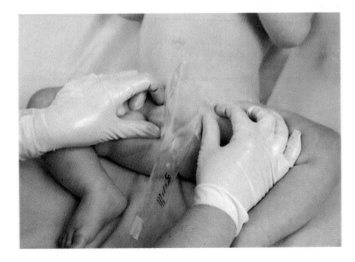

**FIGURE 26.** Attaching the urine collection bag.

- Make sure the seal is tight to prevent leakage.
- Check the bag frequently for urine.

#### *To Remove a Bag Containing Urine*

- Gently pull the bag away from the skin. Fold the opening over and place the urine bag into the specimen container.
- Cap the container tightly.

## COLLECTING A CLEAN-CATCH URINE SPECIMEN (OLDER CHILD)

### Selected Equipment

Towelettes
Sterile urine specimen container

### Procedure

#### *Male*

- After washing his hands, instruct the older child to clean the head of his penis (after pulling back the foreskin, if not circumcised) three times, each time using a different towelette, moving from the urethral meatus outward.
- Have the child urinate a small amount into the toilet, stop the flow, then urinate into the sterile container.
- Cap the container tightly.

#### *Female*

- After washing her hands, instruct the child to sit back on the toilet as far as possible with her legs apart. Have her spread her labia with her fingers and wipe each side with a separate towelette using a front-to-back stroke. Tell the child to use a third wipe to clean the meatus, repeating the front-to-back motion.
- Have the child urinate a small amount into the toilet, stop the flow, then urinate into the sterile container.
- Cap the container tightly.

# ▶ STOOL CULTURE

Stool cultures are used to detect the presence of undesirable bacteria in the intestinal tract. A sample for culture can be obtained from stool collected in a cup, from a diaper, or from a swab that has been gently inserted into the child's rectum.

## OBTAINING A STOOL SPECIMEN

### Selected Equipment

Two culturette swabs

### Procedure—*Clean Gloves*

- Open one culturette swab, holding it in your dominant hand while keeping the tube and cover in your nondominant hand.
- Dip the swab into the stool. Place the swab in the culturette tube and cover. Squeeze the bottom of the closed culturette to release the culture medium.
- Repeat with the second culturette.

# ► WOUND CULTURE

A culturette swab is used to obtain samples for microscopic examination from a wound or body site such as the eyes, ears, nose, throat, rectum, or vagina.

## OBTAINING A SAMPLE FOR WOUND CULTURE

### Selected Equipment

One culturette swab

### Procedure—*Sterile Gloves*

- Open the culturette, holding it in your dominant hand while keeping the tube and cover in your nondominant hand.
- Gently swab the infected area.
- Place the swab in the culturette tube and release the culture medium.

# ► THROAT CULTURE

A culturette swab is used to obtain a sample from the throat for microscopic examination.

## OBTAINING A SAMPLE FOR A THROAT CULTURE

### Selected Equipment

Two culturette swabs

### Procedure—*Clean Gloves*

- Open the culturette, holding it in your dominant hand while keeping the cover in your nondominant hand.
- Gently swab the back of the throat along each tonsillar area with a separate culturette.
- Place the swab in the culturette tube and release the culture medium.

# ▶ RESPIRATORY SECRETIONS

Secretions are obtained to detect bacteria that cause respiratory infections. Different techniques are used for infants and older children. The infant will need suctioning. The older child can cooperate and cough into the container provided.

## COLLECTING RESPIRATORY SECRETIONS FROM AN INFANT

### Selected Equipment

Sterile suction catheter
Sterile normal saline
Suction trap

### Procedure—*Sterile Gloves*

- According to the manufacturer's guidelines, attach the suction trap to low wall suction (60 mm Hg).
- Suction the child's nose (refer to the description of suctioning in Unit 9), using a small amount of sterile normal saline to clear the tubing.
- Close the trap.

*Note:* This will provide a specimen from the nasopharyngeal area. If a tracheal specimen is needed, the deep suctioning technique described in Unit 9 should be consulted.

## COLLECTING RESPIRATORY SECRETIONS FROM A CHILD

FIGURE 27. Obtaining a sputum specimen.

### Selected Equipment

Sterile specimen container

### Procedure—*Clean Gloves*

- Encourage the child to take several deep breaths, then cough sputum up and spit it into the cup (Fig. 27).
- Close the cup.

# ADMINISTRATION OF MEDICATION 7

Administering medications to children presents a number of challenges: deciding which drugs to use, determining dosages, choosing methods and sites, and taking into account implications based on the child's development.

Although the drug and the dosage are determined by the prescriber, it is imperative that the nurse observe the "Five Rights" of medication administration (Table 4) before any medication is given.

Explain all procedures or treatments to the child and parents, based on the child's developmental stage and the level of understanding of both parties. Answer all questions before giving the medication. Identify any known drug allergies.

## 4 | "Five Rights" of Medication Administration

1. Right medication
   - Compare the name of the drug on the medication sheet with the name of the drug on the label of the drug container three times. Check the container's expiration date.
   - Know the action of the drug.
   - Identify the potential side effects of the drug.
   - Use the pharmacy, hospital, or other drug formulary as a reference for medications with which you are unfamiliar.
2. Right patient
   - Verify the name on the medication sheet against the name on the child's identification band. When in a setting with no name band (eg, clinic), verify the child's name with the child and parent by asking them to state the name.
3. Right time
   - When ordered for a specific time, a medication should be given within 20–30 minutes of that time.
   - For prn medications, check the last time the dose was given as well as the total 24-hour dose the child has received to verify that the child can receive another dose at this time.
4. Right route of administration
   - Always use the ordered route for administration of a medication. If a change is needed (such as a change from oral medication when a child is vomiting), check with the prescriber to get an order for a change in route.
5. Right dose
   - Calculate the ordered dose based on the child's weight in kilograms.
   - If in doubt about what constitutes an appropriate dose, compare to the pharmacy, hospital, or other drug formulary guidelines for recommended dose.
   - Question the order if the dose is outside of recommended amounts.

---

### SAMPLE DOCUMENTATION

September 6, 1998, 1400 hours: 250 mg (1 mL) ceftriaxone injected into the right deltoid. No redness, swelling noted. September 6, 1998, 1420 hours: No reaction to medication noted at this time. Vital signs stable (see flowsheet). Patient discharged to home with instructions to return immediately if he has difficulty breathing or the area becomes red, painful, or swollen.

When a medication is given, record the name of the drug, the route, the date and time, and, if appropriate, the site. It is often necessary to record the response to the medication, including desired effects and undesired side effects. This is especially important with medications for pain control and those for treatment of an acute problem such as respiratory difficulty.

## ▶ ORAL MEDICATION

Children younger than 5 years of age usually have difficulty swallowing tablets and capsules. For this reason, most medications for pediatric use are also available in the form of elixirs, syrups, or suspensions. If a medication is available only in tablet or capsule form, it may need to be crushed before being administered. Be sure not to crush medications with enteric coating. Remember to wear clean gloves if your hands might come in contact with the child's saliva.

## ADMINISTERING AN ORAL MEDICATION

### Preparation

- Measure the medication accurately to ensure that the dose is correct.
- If the oral medication is liquid (especially if less than 5 mL), it should be measured in a syringe or calibrated small medicine cup or dropper. A specially designed medication bottle may also be used (Fig. 28).
- Choose the appropriate device from those available to administer an oral liquid medication (Fig. 28).

FIGURE 28. Oral medications can be administered with various types of equipment, depending on the child's age.

- If a tablet or pill needs to be crushed, place it in a mortar or between two paper medicine cups and crush it with a pestle. Once the tablet or pill has been pulverized, mix the powdered medication with a small amount of flavored substance such as juice, applesauce, or jelly to disguise any unpleasant flavor.

### Selected Equipment

Medicine cup, syringe, or other device for administering medication
Medication

### Procedure

#### Infant

- A syringe or dropper provides the best control.
- Place small amounts of liquid along the side of the infant's mouth. To prevent aspiration or spitting out, wait for the infant to swallow before giving more.
- *Alternative method:* Have the infant suck the liquid through a nipple.

#### Toddler or Young Child

- Place the child firmly on your lap or the parent's lap in a sitting or modified supine position (Fig. 29).
- Administer the medication slowly with a syringe or small medicine cup.

FIGURE 29. This father needs to administer a medication to his daughter at home. He has been instructed how to hold her and administer the dose safely and effectively.

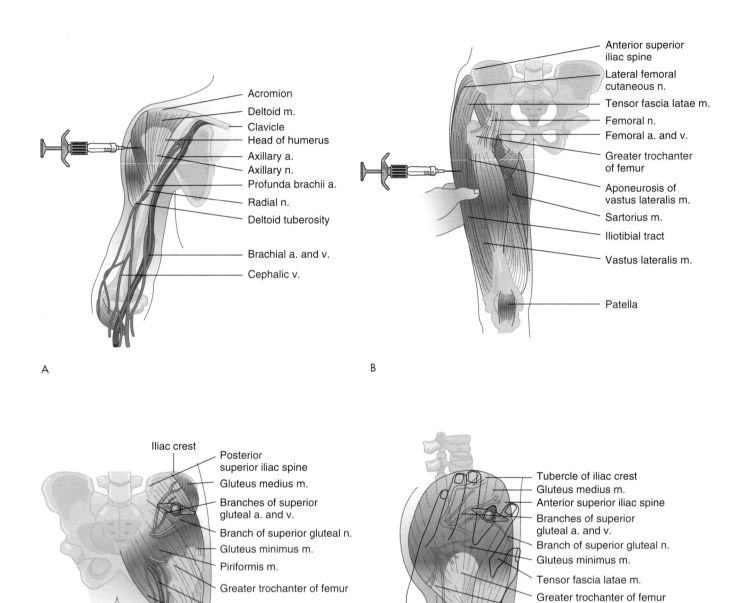

**FIGURE 30.** Intramuscular injection sites. **A,** Deltoid. **B,** Vastus lateralis. **C,** Dorsogluteal. **D,** Ventrogluteal.
*Redrawn and modified from Bindler, R., & Howry, L. (1997). Pediatric drugs and nursing implications (2nd ed., pp. 39–42). Stamford, CT: Appleton & Lange.*

# ▶ INTRAMUSCULAR INJECTION

The site of the intramuscular injection (Fig. 30) depends on the age of the child, the amount of muscle mass, and the density and volume of medication to be administered. Young infants may not tolerate volumes greater than 0.5 mL in a single site, whereas older infants or small children may be able to tolerate 1 mL per site. As the child grows, greater volumes can be administered. Remember: The larger the volume of medication, the larger the muscle to be used. If possible, avoid areas that involve major blood vessels or nerves.

The preferred site for the infant is the vastus lateralis muscle (Fig. 31), which lies along the mid-anterior lateral aspect of the thigh. After the child has been walking for 1 year, the dorsogluteal site can be used. However, since that muscle is poorly developed, it is not the ideal choice for a child less than 5 years old.

For the older child and adolescent, the sites are the same as for the adult: the vastus lateralis, deltoid, and ventrogluteal muscles.

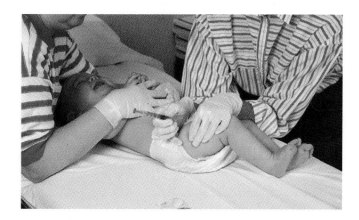

FIGURE 31. In infants, the vastus lateralis muscle is preferred for intramuscular injections.

## ADMINISTERING AN INTRAMUSCULAR INJECTION

**FIGURE 32.** The child should be restrained by the parent or an assistant during intramuscular injection.

### Preparation

- Select the syringe size according to the volume and dose of medication to be delivered. The needle must be long enough to penetrate the subcutaneous tissue and enter the muscle. Needles with a length of 0.5–1 inch (25 to 21 gauge) are recommended for infants and children.
- Choose the appropriate site (see the preceding discussion).

### Selected Equipment

Syringe filled with medication

### Procedure—*Clean Gloves*

- Have another nurse, an assistant, or the parent restrain the child during the injection (Fig. 32).
- Locate the site. Clean with alcohol using an outward circular motion.
- Grasp the muscle between your thumb and fingers for stabilization.
- Remove the cap from the syringe. Insert the needle quickly at a 90-degree angle. Pull back the plunger.
- If no blood is aspirated, inject the medication, withdraw the needle, massage the area with a gauze pad (alcohol will sting), and return the child to a position of comfort.
- Do not recap the needle. Discard it in a puncture-resistant container according to standard precaution recommendations.

# ► SUBCUTANEOUS INJECTION

The site of the subcutaneous injection depends on the age of the child. Usually the dorsum of the upper arm or the anterior thigh is used in newborns, infants, and toddlers. The upper arm is the most commom site for older children.

## ADMINISTERING A SUBCUTANEOUS INJECTION

### Preparation

- Select the syringe size based on the volume or dose of medication to be delivered. The needle must be just long enough to penetrate the subcutaneous tissue, which lies below the skin and fat surface and above the muscle. Needles with a length of ⅜ to ⅝ inch (26 to 25 gauge) are recommended for infants and children.
- Choose the appropriate site (see the preceding discussion).

### Selected Equipment

Syringe filled with medication

### Procedure—*Clean Gloves*

- Have another nurse, an assistant, or the parent restrain the child while the injection is being given.
- Locate the site. Clean with alcohol using an outward circular motion.
- Pinch the skin between your thumb and index finger.
- Remove the cap from the syringe. Insert the needle quickly at about a 45-degree angle. Release the skin and pull back the plunger.
- If no blood is aspirated, inject the medication, withdraw the needle at the angle at which it was inserted, massage the area with a gauze pad (alcohol will sting), and return the child to a position of comfort.
- Do not recap the needle. Discard it in a puncture-resistant container according to standard precaution recommendations.

## ► INTRAVENOUS MEDICATION

The principles of intravenous (IV) medication administration in children are the same as those in adults. Special considerations when administering IV medication are discussed in this section.

Assess the IV line for patency. Remember that the effect of most IV medications is almost immediate. If you are administering narcotics or benzodiazepines, have antagonists and ventilation equipment at the bedside.

Many drugs have specific dilution recommendations. Some medications are compatible only with specific fluids such as normal saline. Other medications must be given very slowly. Still other drugs can be administered quickly. Know your institution's or pharmacy's standards for IV push (less than 10 minutes) versus intermittent medication administration. Be sure you know which medications are incompatible with one another. Flush the IV line between administrations. See Unit 8 for administration of intravenous medications.

## SPECIAL CONSIDERATIONS

It is recommended that IV medications for infants and children be put in a volume control chamber such as a Soluset or Metriset with the diluent and placed on an electronic pump for accurate administration. Set the pump for the volume to be infused and the rate of infusion. Flush the line after the infusion to ensure that all medication has been administered, since some medication will remain in the distal tubing.

Some medications can be given as a bolus, by injecting the drug directly into a port of the IV tubing. Check with your pharmacy, the manufacturer's insert, or a medication resource book for recommendations about which port to use, distal or proximal to the child, and the rate of infusion.

## ► OPHTHALMIC MEDICATION

Young children fear having anything placed in their eyes, and special care is often needed to reduce the child's anxiety and promote cooperation during instillation of ophthalmic medications. An explanation of the procedure may help gain the child's cooperation. To prevent the transfer of pathogens to the eye, the medication and its dispensing port must be kept sterile.

## ADMINISTERING AN OPHTHALMIC MEDICATION

### Selected Equipment

Medication

### Procedure—*Clean Gloves*

- Have another nurse, an assistant, or the parent restrain the child in a supine position with the child's head extended.
- Use your nondominant hand to pull the child's lower lid down while your other hand rests on the child's head (Fig. 33).

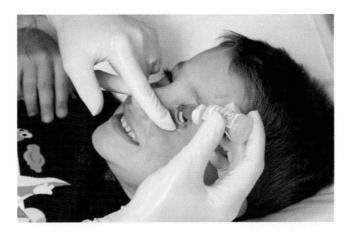

FIGURE 33. Administering an ophthalmic medication. The child is instructed to close the eyes and pretend to look up toward his head. The nurse then gently retracts the lower lid and inserts the medication.

- Instill the drops or ointment into the conjunctival sac that has formed.
- *Alternative method:* Pull the lower lid out far enough to form a reservoir in which the medication can be instilled.
- After the medication has been instilled, close the child's eyelids to prevent leakage.
- Have the child lie quietly for a minimum of 30 seconds. Discourage the child from squeezing the eyes shut.
- Dry the inner canthus of the eye.
- Keep the child's head in the midline position to prevent the medication from contaminating the other eye.

## ► OTIC MEDICATION

Otic medications, which are available in liquid form, are placed in the external ear canal using a dropper. Otic drops are sometimes applied to soften cerumen, enabling it to be cleansed from the canal. The ear canal is not treated with sterile technique unless the tympanic membrane is ruptured and draining.

## ADMINISTERING AN OTIC MEDICATION

### Selected Equipment

Medication
Cotton ball

### Procedure—*Clean Gloves*

- Have another nurse, an assistant, or the parent restrain the child in a supine position with the head turned as appropriate for administration (Fig. 34).

FIGURE 34. Administering an otic medication.

- *For the child less than 3 years of age:* Gently pull the pinna straight back and downward to straighten the ear canal.
- *For the older child:* Pull the pinna back and upward.
- When the pinna is in the proper position, instill the drops into the ear.
- Keep the child in the same position for a few minutes. Gently rub the area just anterior to the ear to facilitate drainage of the medication into the ear canal. If desired, a cotton ball may be loosely placed in the ear to promote retention of the medication.

# ► NASAL MEDICATION

Medications instilled into the nares drain into the back of the mouth and throat, and may cause sensations of difficulty in breathing, tickling, or bad taste. After instillation of the drops, the child should be observed for choking or vomiting. Saline nose drops are sometimes given to young infants who have respiratory disorders to clear the nasal passages.

## ADMINISTERING A NASAL MEDICATION

### Selected Equipment

Medication

### Procedure—*Clean Gloves*

- Place the child in a supine position with the head hyperextended over the parent's lap or over the edge of the examination table or bed.
- Instill the drops into the nostrils.
- Keep the child in the same position for at least 5 minutes to allow the medication to contact the nasal mucosa.

## ▶ AEROSOL THERAPY

Aerosol therapy is used when medication needs to be deposited directly into the airway. Bronchodilators, steroids, and antibiotics can be administered to children in aerosol form. Several methods are used to provide aerosol therapy, such as intermittent positive pressure breathing machines and nebulizers. The most common aerosol therapy for children is the metered dose inhaler (MDI) commonly used in treatment of asthma (see Chapter 11 of Ball and Bindler's *Pediatric Nursing* for a description of this treatment for asthma). Because nebulizers are the type of aerosol treatment commonly used in the hospital and administered by nurses, their use is also described here.

## ADMINISTERING NEBULIZER AEROSOL THERAPY

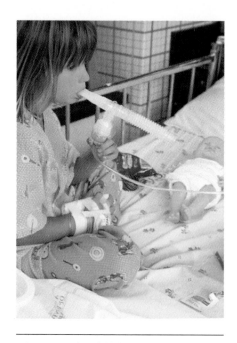

**FIGURE 35.** This child has been taught to use a nebulizer for treatment of her asthma in the hospital. After explanation and demonstration by the nurse, she now independently and effectively completes the treatment.

### Preparation

- The dose of the medication is based on the child's weight. The medication is placed in the cup of the aerosol kit; 2–3 mL of normal saline can be added as a diluent if ordered.
- Perform a baseline assessment, including heart and respiratory rates, breath sounds, and respiratory effort.

### Selected Equipment

Reservoir
Mouthpiece or blow-by tubing (depending on child's age)
Portable nebulizing machine or tubing to hook to oxygen supply

### Procedure

- Place the mask on the child.
- Give an assistant or the parent the tubing for blow-by, or have the child put the mouthpiece in his or her mouth (Fig. 35).
- Attach the oxygen tubing to the oxygen flowmeter at 6–7 L/min.
- Have the child take deep breaths during the treatment.
- The aerosol administration should last about 10 minutes. Reassess the child's condition after the therapy.

# ▶ METERED DOSE INHALER

Metered dose inhalers (MDI) are small canister devices with a mouthpiece used to treat asthma in the home setting. They may be used on a regular basis or during times of respiratory distress.

**HOME CARE CONSIDERATIONS**

When a child is using a metered dose inhaler, observe the child's self-administration technique on occasional home visits and office visits. Offer teaching to improve the use and effectiveness of the inhaler, if needed. Record your observations and teaching and follow up on a later visit.

## USING A METERED DOSE INHALER (MDI)

### Selected Equipment

Inhaler with medication

### Procedure

- Insert the canister into the mouthpiece.
- Have the child take a deep breath of room air, inhaling and exhaling completely.
- Ask the child to close the lips tightly over the MDI mouthpiece, and then inhale deeply and slowly through the mouth.
- Depress the canister one time while the child is inhaling; one dose of medication will be inhaled.
- Have the child hold his or her breath for about 5–10 seconds to enable medication to reach the lungs.
- MDIs may have reservoirs, spacers, or extenders for those children who have difficulty holding their breath long enough or closing their mouths securely over the mouthpiece.

## ▶ RECTAL MEDICATION

Rectal administration is sometimes used when the oral route is contraindicated. Although absorption is less reliable than with oral preparations, many medications, such as acetaminophen, aspirin, antiemetics, analgesics, and sedatives, come in suppository form.

## ADMINISTERING A RECTAL MEDICATION

### Selected Equipment

Water-soluble lubricant
Suppository

### Preparation

If the suppository is to be halved, cut it lengthwise.

### Procedure—*Clean Gloves*

- Have another nurse, an assistant, or the parent hold the child in a side-lying or (if small enough) a prone position on the parent's lap.
- Slightly lubricate the tapered tip of the suppository. Using either the index finder (in children over 3 years of age) or the little finger (in infants and toddlers), gently insert the suppository into the child's rectum, just beyond the internal sphincter.
- Hold the buttocks together for 5–10 minutes, until the urge to expel the medication has passed.

# ► CALCULATION OF MEDICATION DOSAGES

It is the nurse's responsibility to calculate the dosage of the medication ordered to determine if the dosage is within the normal range for the child's height and weight.

Dosages can be calculated using the child's weight (written as mg/kg) or total body surface area. Body surface area is determined by plotting the child's height and weight on a nomogram (see Appendix E). Draw a line connecting the two columns and note the results at the point where the drawn lines cross the center column. The dosage is ordered as $mg/m^2$.

## Example 1

The physician orders morphine (10 mg/mL) for a 3-year-old child who weighs 15 kg. The recommended dose for children is 0.1 mg/kg. What dose is appropriate for the child's weight? How much volume should be drawn?

## Answer

$$\text{Recommended dose} \times \text{Weight} = \text{Dose for patient}$$
$$0.1 \text{ mg/kg} \times 15 \text{ kg} = 1.5 \text{ mg}$$

$$\frac{\text{Dose desired}}{\text{Dose on hand}} \times \text{Quantity in mL} = \text{Volume to be administered}$$

$$\frac{1.5 \text{ mg}}{10 \text{ mg}} \times 1 \text{ mL} = 0.15 \text{ mL to be administered}$$

## Example 2

The physician orders phenobarbital (65 mg/mL) for a 5-year-old child who weighs 20 kg. The recommended loading dose for the child is 10–20 mg/kg. The physician orders 250 mg to be infused over 30 minutes. Is this dose appropriate for the child's weight? How much volume should be administered? How do you set the infusion pump?

## Answer

$$\text{Recommended dose} \times \text{Weight} = \text{Desired dose}$$
$$\frac{10 \text{ mg}}{\text{kg}} \times 20 \text{ kg} = 200 \text{ mg}$$
$$\frac{20 \text{ mg}}{\text{kg}} \times 20 \text{ kg} = 400 \text{ mg}$$

Dose of 250 mg is within recommended range.

$$\frac{\text{Dose desired}}{\text{Dose on hand}} \times \text{Quantity in mL} = \text{Volume to be administered}$$

$$\frac{250 \text{ mg}}{65 \text{ mg}} \times 1 \text{ mL} = 3.85 \text{ mL}$$

## Pump Setup

The nurse determines that the volume for the setup is 50 mL.

$$\frac{50 \text{ mL}}{30 \text{ min}} \times \frac{60 \text{ min}}{1 \text{ hr}} = \frac{100 \text{ mL}}{\text{hr}}$$
$$\text{Rate} = 100 \text{ mL/hr}$$

# INTRAVENOUS ACCESS 8

## ▶ PERIPHERAL VASCULAR ACCESS

In both infants and children, veins of the extremities are used for venous access. Scalp veins may also be used in infants.

Over-the-needle catheters (19–27 gauge) are preferred for infants and children. The size of the catheter is determined by the size of the child and the size of the vein. For example, a 24-gauge catheter is used for a newborn; a 20–22-gauge catheter is used for an older infant, toddler, or school-aged child. A butterfly needle (23 gauge) may be used in certain situations, such as when accessing a scalp vein in an infant. Use of a butterfly needle should be considered a temporary measure, with continued effort made to achieve more stable and secure venous access.

## CHOICE OF SITE

### Scalp

Scalp veins are used when other access cannot be obtained (Fig. 36). Protect the site by covering it with a plastic medication cup secured with tape.

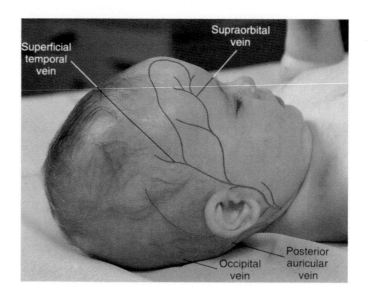

FIGURE 36. Scalp veins are frequently used for peripheral vascular access in infants.

### Extremities

Veins of the antecubital fossa or forearm are usually the best sites for venous access because they are highly visible; however, the dorsum of the hand and foot also may be used.

#### Special Considerations

- Avoid using the foot veins as a site in children who are walking.
- Avoid using the child's dominant hand or the hand used by an infant for finger sucking or blanket holding.
- If two sites are needed, do not use both antecubital veins because the child will be rendered helpless.
- Use padded armboards as splints to decrease mobility of the extremity.
- Use gauze under tape or tape over tape to decrease skin contact with adhesive tape.

## ACCESSING A PERIPHERAL VEIN

### Preparation

- Place and maintain the child in a supine position with the help of an assistant. Have the person assisting you lean over the child to control the child's body and extend the extremity to be used. An alternative to human restraint is to use a papoose board (see the use of a papoose, in Unit 2).
- If a scalp vein is to be used, place a rubber band around the infant's head to serve as a tourniquet to distend the veins. If the extremities are to be used, place the tourniquet proximal to the desired vein to distend it. If necessary, hold the extremity below heart level, gently rub or tap the vein, or apply a warm compress to promote dilation of the vein.
- Locate the vein by inspection (wiping with alcohol will make the vein shine) or palpation.
- If you are using an extremity, apply an armboard or footboard. Relocate the vein.
- *If using the antecubital fossa:* Slightly hyperextend the child's elbow and pronate the arm. Secure the arm to the armboard by applying tape above the elbow and at the wrist.
- *If using the dorsum of the hand:* Place the child's hand on the armboard, palmar side down, with the fingers wrapped around the distal edge (Fig. 37). Apply tape over the fingers, then around the thumb separately. Next apply tape at the wrist. A gauze roll may be placed under the wrist to increase flexion.

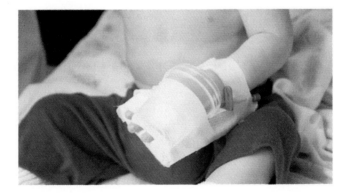

**FIGURE 37.** This intravenous site on a hand has been placed on an armboard, securely wrapped, and covered with part of a plastic cup to prevent the child from disrupting the line.

- *If using the foot:* Apply the footboard to the child's foot, which is dorsiflexed. Apply tape across the toes, instep, and ankle. Use gauze as needed under the lateral malleolus.

## Selected Equipment

Tourniquet
Alcohol or povidone–iodine
Different sized armboards
IV catheter (depends on size of vein)
T connector that has been flushed and attached to normal saline–filled syringe
IV tubing and bag with solution

## Procedure—*Clean Gloves*

- Clean the skin with alcohol or povidone–iodine using an outward circular motion. Let each area dry before continuing. Apply the tourniquet. Hold the skin taut, gently pulling with your thumb just distal to the site of the puncture.
- Puncture the skin with the catheter, with the bevel side up, positioned at a 15 degree angle and aimed at the vein in the direction of the blood flow. When blood appears, gently slide the catheter into the vein. Release the tourniquet. Remove the stylette.
- Attach the normal saline–filled T connector and attempt to flush the catheter. If it flushes easily, tape the catheter in place, using a V pattern around the catheter itself. Further secure the catheter with gauze and tape (taking care not to cover the area proximal to the site completely). Alternately, a transparent dressing can be used over the site to allow for observation for signs of infiltration or phlebitis.
- Write the date, time, catheter size, and your initials on a piece of tape and place it on the dressing.
- The T connector can be hooked up to a heparin lock or used immediately for fluid or medication infusion.

---

# MEDICATION LOCK (HEPARIN LOCK)

The medication lock (formerly called a heparin lock) is a small device placed on the IV catheter and taped in place. It maintains the IV site for future use when not hooked up to a running IV infusion. Some agencies use normal saline while some use of heparin solution to maintain patency of medication locks. Know and follow your agency policy.

## ATTACHING A MEDICATION LOCK CAP TO AN IV INFUSION

### Selected Equipment

Syringe filled with 1 mL of prepackaged heparin flush solution (10 U/mL) or normal saline
Syringe with 2 mL of sterile normal saline
Luer-lok male adapter

### Procedure—*Clean Gloves*

- Prime the adaptor (fill it, being sure to prevent air pockets) with the heparin flush solution or saline, according to agency policy.
- Save the rest of the flush solution to use when the lock is inserted into the IV tubing.
- Be sure the IV line is securely taped in place (Fig. 38A). Check the patency of the IV tubing by flushing with 2 mL of sterile normal saline. Be sure there is no redness, swelling, pallor, coolness, or pain at the IV site.

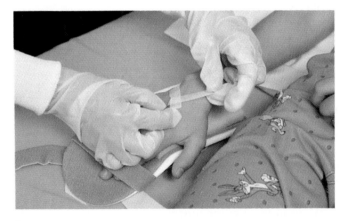
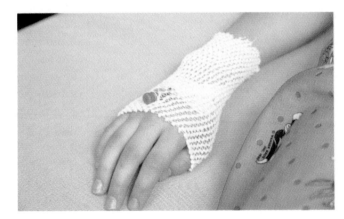

A                                                                B

FIGURE 38. **A,** Taping the IV line for placement of a medication lock. **B,** Medication lock in place.

- Clamp the T connector on the IV line to prevent outflow of blood.
- Remove the IV tubing from the line and quickly place a primed catheter cap on the T connector.
- Open the clamp. Insert the medication flush solution and slowly flush the adaptor.
- Remove the syringe and clamp the medication lock.
- Secure the medication lock with tape and cover with an elastic bandage (Fig. 38B).
- Flush the line every 8 hours with normal saline or heparin flush solution, as determined by your agency policy.

## INFUSING MEDICATION: MEDICATION LOCK IN PLACE

### Selected Equipment

Alcohol swabs
19–27-gauge needle or needleless system
Two syringes filled with 2 mL of normal saline with 19–27-gauge needles or needleless system
Medication ordered
Syringe with 1 mL of heparin flush solution (10 U/mL) or normal saline

### Procedure—*Clean Gloves*

- Clean the catheter cap with alcohol. Unclamp the heparin lock.
- Check the patency of the IV tubing by flushing it with normal saline. Check the catheter tip site for swelling.
- If the IV line is patent and operating, apply the new syringe or needleless system on the distal end of the IV tubing through the cap after cleaning its surface. Recessed needles or needleless systems are recommended whenever available.
- Secure the IV tubing and connection area in place with tape.
- Administer the infusion of medication according to the prescriber's orders.
- Be sure to follow the infusion with 10–20 mL of IV fluid so no medication remains in the tubing.
- After completion of the infusion, discard used equipment into a puncture-proof container according to standard precaution recommendations.
- If the IV tubing is to be used again, cover it with a clean needle system to ensure sterility.
- Clean the catheter cap with alcohol.
- Flush first with 2 mL of normal saline and then with the heparin flush solution if heparin is used. Clamp the heparin lock and secure it in place.

## ADMINISTERING AN IV PUSH BOLUS OF MEDICATION: MEDICATION LOCK IN PLACE

### Selected Equipment

Alcohol swabs

Two 1–2-mL syringes filled with normal saline with 19–25-gauge needles or needleless system

Syringe filled with 1 mL of heparin flush solution (10 U/mL) or normal saline

Medication in syringe covered with 19–25-gauge needle

### Procedure—*Clean Gloves*

- Clean the catheter cap with alcohol. Unclamp the lock.
- Pierce the catheter cap with a normal saline–filled syringe.
- Flush the line with 2 mL of normal saline to check patency.
- Remove the syringe and needle.
- Insert the medication syringe through the catheter cap and give the medication according to the prescriber's orders. Check a medication resource book or call your hospital pharmacy to determine the rate of administration. When all of the medication has been administered, remove the syringe.
- Flush the line with the 2 mL of normal saline, followed by the heparin flush solution if heparin is used. Clamp and secure the line.
- Discard the equipment in a puncture-proof container according to standard precaution recommendations.

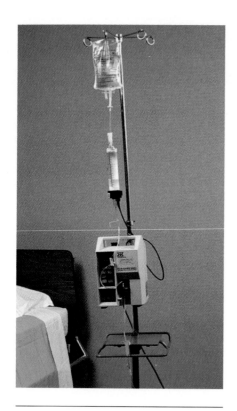

**FIGURE 39.** IV setup with infusion pump.

## ▶ INTRAVENOUS INFUSION

### FLUID ADMINISTRATION

The amount of fluid to be administered to a child is based on the child's weight and pathophysiologic state. It is recommended that fluids be given to the infant or child through an infusion pump (Fig. 39), because this device allows for a more accurate setting of flow rates than gravity does. Maintenance fluid requirements are based on the child's weight (see Table 5).

| 5 Pediatric Maintenance Fluid Requirements | |
| --- | --- |
| **Weight (kg)** | **Fluid Requirements** |
| 0–10 | 100 mL/kg/24 hr |
| 10–20 | 1000 mL + 50 mL/kg/24 hr for each kg between 11 and 20 |
| 20–70 | 1500 mL + 20 mL/kg/24 hr for each kg between 21 and 70 |
| Over 70 | 2500 mL/24 hr (adult requirement) |

### Pumps

An infusion pump can be used to control the administration of small volumes of fluid, blood, medication, and total parenteral nutrition. A smaller syringe pump (Fig. 40) can be attached directly to the lowest port on the IV tubing for immediate infusion of medication.

It is important to be familiar with the type of infusion pump used at your institution. Be sure to set controls for both the amount of fluid to be infused and the rate of infusion. Check the pump frequently to be certain it is programmed and working correctly.

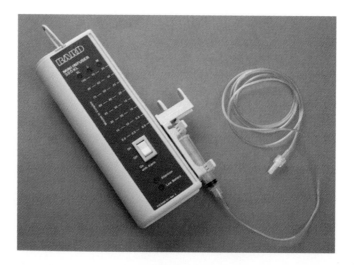

**FIGURE 40.** Syringe pump.

## Preparation for Hanging Fluids

Before hanging any fluids, check the bag or bottle for leaks, expiration date, impurities, or color changes. Verify the order for type of solution and rate of infusion. Obtain the tape necessary if used to mark bags for infusion speed.

Select tubing for either a pump or gravity drip. Make sure that the tubing is clamped off. Remove the protective covering from the insertion piece (spike). Place the insertion piece into the entry port of the bag or bottle. Invert the bag or bottle and hang it on a pole. Pinch the drip chamber (it should be no more than one half full). Direct the distal end of the tubing into a clean receptacle, maintaining sterility of the end. Open the clamp and let the fluid run through the length of the tubing. Tap the tubing at each port to remove any trapped air. Close the clamp, recap the sterile end, and check the entire length of tubing for air bubbles. The tubing is now primed and ready for use.

If a volume control chamber (Soluset or Metriset) is used, first attach it to the bag or bottle. Close the clamp that is closest to the fluid and the one that is distal to the chamber. Open the top clamp. Let about 50 mL into the chamber and then close the clamp. Pinch the drip chamber as above. Open the distal clamp, and continue to purge the tubing (as described above).

If you are using a pump, check the manufacturer's guidelines for purging the tubing.

## Guidelines for Infusion of IV Fluids

Rules for determining flow rate for instilling IV fluids via gravity are based on the drip factor of the IV tubing being used.

## Microdrip Tubing

| Manufacturer | Drops/mL |
|---|---|
| All major manufacturers | 60 drops (gtt) = 1 mL |

## Formula

$$mL/hr = gtt/min$$

## Example

$$1000 \text{ mL}/8 \text{ hr} = 125 \text{ mL/hr} = 125 \text{ gtt/min}$$

## Macrodrip Tubing

| Manufacturer | Drops/mL |
|---|---|
| AVI | 20 gtt = 1 mL |
| McGaw/Abbot | 15 gtt = 1 mL |
| Travenol | 10 gtt = 1 mL |

## Formula

Total volume × Drop factor/Infusion time in minutes = Drops/minute

## Example

$$1000 \text{ mL} \times 10 \text{ (Travenol)}/8 \text{ hr } (480 \text{ min}) = 21 \text{ gtt/min}$$

**NURSING ALERT**

Blood is administered according to the physician's orders. However, a bag should never remain hanging longer than 4 hours. Do not use the blood line for any other infusions. If a medication must be administered by that line, turn off the infusion, flush the line with normal saline, administer the medication, flush the line again with normal saline, and then restart the blood infusion.

## BLOOD ADMINISTRATION

To safely administer blood or blood products to the infant or child, be aware of the protocols followed at your institution. Check to be sure that an informed consent for administration is present in the chart. Since hypersensitivity reactions can occur and other side effects can be severe, administration of blood is approached with many nursing cautions. Be sure to take vital signs and monitor the child closely. Follow instructions from the blood bank and other resources for correct administration of blood products, such as frozen plasma, cryoprecipitate, and clotting factors.

## ADMINISTERING BLOOD OR BLOOD PRODUCTS

### Preparation

- Identify the bag to be used and compare it with the requisition (type, Rh factor, patient number, blood donor number) and the child's identification bracelet. Do this step with another nurse at the bedside. Both nurses are responsible for signing the slips as the transfusers.
- Check the blood for any bubbles, dark areas, or sediment.
- Ask the child or family about previous transfusions, especially any history of allergic reactions.
- Take the child's vital signs, including pulse, respiratory rate, temperature, and blood pressure.
- When estimating preparation time, keep in mind that blood must be hung within 20–30 minutes after being removed from the blood bank refrigerator. For trauma patients who need massive transfusions, the bag should be warmed to 37°C (99°F) (only an approved blood warmer should be used).
- Use the correct tubing for the blood product being administered. A Y blood administration set is preferred. If a Y setup is used, hang normal saline at the extra connector.

### Selected Equipment

Blood product
Y tubing and bag of normal saline
Normal saline flush solution
Sterile needle or needleless system
Intravenous line in place with 18-gauge needle or larger

### Procedure—*Clean Gloves*

- Take the child's baseline vital signs.
- Verify the type and crossmatch data on the blood with another registered nurse.
- Attach the blood bag to one end of the Y tubing. Flush the line with normal saline attached to the other side of the Y tubing.

- Clamp off the tubing, keeping the distal end covered.
- Disconnect it, covering the hub with a sterile needle or needleless system to keep it sterile. Flush the child's IV line with normal saline to ensure its patency.
- Attach the blood tubing.
- Slowly open the clamp on tubing, adjusting the flow with the roller. Start the transfusion slowly.
- The flow rate may be increased if no reaction is noted. (Most reactions occur within 20 minutes.)
- Closely monitor the child's vital signs and response. Vital signs should be taken every 5 minutes for the first 15 minutes, every 15 minutes during the first hour, then hourly until the transfusion is complete (*or* follow your hospital's protocol).
- If the child develops any sign of a transfusion reaction (Table 6), stop the transfusion, change the IV to normal saline, and notify the physician immediately.

**HOME CARE CONSIDERATIONS**

When a child receives a transfusion of blood or blood products, administration of immunizations must be delayed for several months afterward (the amount of time is dependent on the particular product used). Be sure to let parents know and provide in writing the type of product used (whole blood, packed red cells, frozen plasma, etc), and the date of the infusion. Instruct them to take this with them when they next visit their regular care provider so that adaptations in immunization administration may be implemented, if needed.

 **6  Transfusion Reactions**

| Type of Reaction | Cause | Description |
|---|---|---|
| Allergic | Caused by immune response to protein in blood | Signs and symptoms may include rash, itching, urticaria, wheezing, laryngospasm, edema, and/or anaphylaxis |
| Febrile or septic | Usually a result of contamination of blood; may also be caused by idiopathic conditions | Signs and symptoms include chills, fever, headache, decreased blood pressure, nausea and/or vomiting, and leg or back pain |
| Hemolytic | Caused by incompatibility of child's blood with donor blood, history of multiple transfusions, or infusion with a solution containing dextrose or other additives | Signs and symptoms include anxiety or restlessness, fever, chills, chest pain, cyanosis, change in vital signs with increased heart and respiratory rates or with decreased blood pressure and/or hematuria; can progress to shock and anuria if not treated promptly |
| Circulatory overload | Results from infusion of excessive amounts of fluid or too rapid administration | Signs and symptoms include labored breathing, chest or lower back pain, productive cough with rales heard on auscultation, and distended neck veins; central venous pressure may increase |

- After the administration of blood, flush the line with normal saline and connect the IV fluid ordered by the physician. Place the used blood bag and tubing in a plastic bag, seal it, and return it to the blood bank with copies of the transfusion information sheet.
- Document all vital signs, responses, and interventions.

# TOTAL PARENTERAL NUTRITION

Total parenteral nutrition (TPN) is the administration of a nutritionally complete formula into a large central vein. TPN is used for children who cannot tolerate gastrointestinal feeding. Children with disorders such as chronic intestinal obstruction, short bowel syndrome, chronic diarrhea, or tumors may require TPN. (The care of these disorders is discussed in Chapters 14 and 15 of Ball and Bindler's *Pediatric Nursing.*)

Hyperalimentation solutions (TPN as well as lipid emulsions) are delivered by separate pumps and connector tubes. The child who is receiving TPN has a central venous catheter in place. Solutions and tubes need to be changed every 24 hours using strict aseptic technique. Tips and connecting points need to be sterile. Since the hyperalimentation solution needs to be protected from light, the bottle should be covered. Nursing responsibilities when caring for a child receiving TPN are outlined in Table 7.

## 7 │ Caring for the Child Receiving TPN

- Monitor intake and output. Changes may indicate fluid and electrolyte disturbances.
- Weigh the child daily.
- Assess the IV site. Watch for signs of redness, irritation, or infection. Change the dressing according to hospital protocol (see the procedure for managing a central venous catheter site in this unit).
- Use the infusion site only for TPN solutions or keep the line open with normal saline. Do not use the line for medications or other infusions.
- Make sure to set each pump correctly, noting the volume and rate of each infusion.
- Check laboratory values, especially glucose, minerals, electrolytes, liver function (bilirubin, alkaline phosphatase), proteins, and triglycerides.
- Note any change in glucose levels:
  1. During the first few days, the high concentration of glucose administration may lead to hyperglycemia. Inform the physician of high blood glucose levels. Insulin may be needed to help the body adjust to the formula.
  2. If hyperalimentation is discontinued abruptly, the child may become hypoglycemic. Be aware of the signs and symptoms of hypoglycemia (see Chapter 20 of Ball and Bindler's *Pediatric Nursing*). Notify the physician if the child's blood glucose level is low.

# ► CENTRAL VENOUS CATHETERS

A central venous catheter is surgically placed when long-term intravenous access is needed, such as for total parenteral nutrition, administration of antibiotics, or chemotherapy. Usually the subclavian vein is accessed and the catheter is threaded into the right atrium. The most common catheter used for children is the Broviac catheter (Fig. 41), which can have a single, double, or triple lumen. Other catheters such as the Hickman may be used with older children. Peripherally inserted central catheter lines (PICC lines) are also common in children.

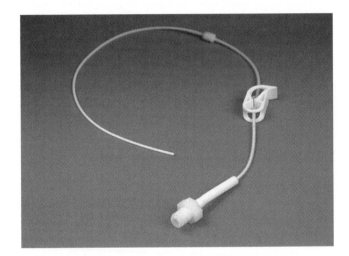

FIGURE 41. Broviac catheter.

## SITE MANAGEMENT

The catheter site is covered with a clear occlusive dressing that should be changed under sterile conditions 2–3 times a week according to agency protocol.

## MANAGING A CENTRAL VENOUS CATHETER SITE

### Selected Equipment

Peroxide-saturated cotton swabs
Alcohol swabs
Providone–iodine swabs
Central venous catheter kit
Sterile occlusive dressing

### Procedure—*Clean Gloves, Sterile Gloves, Mask*

- Open the kit. Don mask and clean gloves.
- Remove the current dressing, working from the edges toward the center. Discard the old dressing and gloves.
- Don the sterile gloves and clean with sterile half-strength peroxide-saturated cotton swabs in an outward circular motion from the point of entry, using one swab for each motion and then changing to a clean one. Clean the area again with alcohol swabs three times, then povidone–iodine swabs, using the same technique.
- Clean the catheter tubing from the exit site to the cap.
- Let dry. Apply antibacterial ointment around the exit site. Place a small sterile gauze over and under the catheter insertion site. Cover with a sterile occlusive dressing.
- Write the date, time, and your initials on a piece of tape and place it on the dressing.

## WITHDRAWING BLOOD

Check the physician's order for the blood tests to be done. It is recommended that the catheter be accessed no more than twice a day.

Have an assistant open and close the clamps as necessary and put the blood in tubes while you are flushing the line.

The double stopcock method of accessing central lines has certain advantages. It is a simple procedure and requires very little setup. The most important feature, however, is that the line is not broken by frequent syringe exchanges as occurs with the direct or single-syringe method. The single-syringe method is described next.

## ACCESSING A CENTRAL VENOUS CATHETER

### Selected Equipment

Sterile 4 × 4 gauze pad
Povidone–iodine solution
Cotton-tipped swabs
Appropriate blood collection tubes
19–20-gauge needles for transferring blood to tubes
Padded clamp (if a clamp is not attached to tubing)

### *For Each Port Accessed:*
Syringe filled with 5–6 mL of normal saline
Syringe filled with 20 mL normal saline
Syringe filled with 2–3 mL of heparin flush solution (10 U/mL)
5–6 mL empty syringe (to draw and discard initial blood)
Syringes for blood samples
Luer-lok or Broviac catheter cap

### Procedure—*Clean Gloves*

- Unpin the catheter from the child's clothes. Remove any tape. Open a sterile 4 × 4 gauze pad to serve as a clean work area. Place the gauze under the catheter connection. If the intravenous solution is infusing, turn it off.
- Clean the connection site with povidine–iodine. Use three swabs, and clean for a total of 2 minutes. Let the connection site dry for an additional 20 seconds.
- Make sure the catheter is clamped. Remove the catheter cap or infusion tubing, maintaining sterility. Flush the catheter with 2–5 mL of normal saline to ensure patency. Slowly aspirate 3–5 mL of blood. Clamp the catheter and discard the syringe. Using another 10-mL syringe, aspirate the amount of blood necessary. Remove the blood-filled syringe and cover with a 19-gauge needle or needleless system. Give that syringe to your assistant to fill the blood collection tubes. Meanwhile, attach the syringe filled with normal saline. Flush the line first with the 20 mL of normal saline, then with the prepared heparin flush solution.
- Clamp the catheter and remove the flush syringe. Connect the infusion solution or cover the port with a sterile protector.
- Secure the catheter to the child's clothing. Remove the gloves and wash your hands.
- Ensure that blood specimens are labeled properly, kept at proper temperature, and transported to the laboratory.

## ROUTINE FLUSHING OF THE LINE

Broviac catheters are flushed once a day, both at home and in the hospital, if they are not accessed. For flushing, 5 mL of heparin flush solution is used.

## ▶ IMPLANTED PORTS

Implanted ports are used most often for children and adolescents who require long-term venous access. The stainless steel port has a self-sealing rubber septum and is surgically implanted under the skin over a bony prominence, most often the clavicle. The catheter is then inserted into the vein that leads to the right atrium. Entry is gained by piercing the skin directly over the port with a specially designed needle (Fig. 42). Sterile gloves, mask, and gown are worn when accessing the site.

The Port-a-Cath is used commonly in pediatrics.

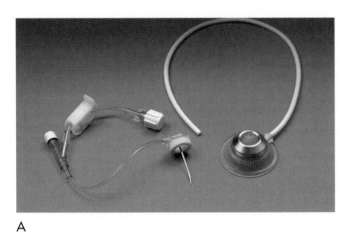

A

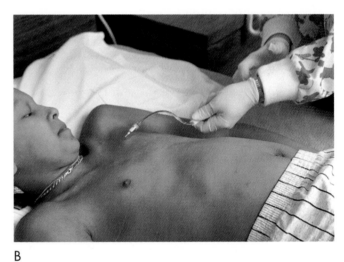

B

FIGURE 42. A, Huber needle. B, Nurse drawing blood from an adolescent who has an implanted port.

# CARDIORESPIRATORY CARE 9

## ►UNIT OUTLINE

ADMINISTRATION OF OXYGEN
  Delivery Systems

OROPHARYNGEAL AIRWAY

NASOPHARYNGEAL AIRWAY

TRACHEOSTOMY
  Tracheostomy Collar
  Tracheostomy Care
  *Performing tracheostomy care*

ENDOTRACHEAL TUBE

VENTILATOR

CARDIOPULMONARY
RESUSCITATION
  Infant
  Child Between 1 and 8 Years

FOREIGN BODY AIRWAY
OBSTRUCTION
  Infant
  Child Between 1 and 8 Years

SUCTIONING
  Nasal/Oral Suctioning
  *Using a bulb syringe*
  *Suctioning a conscious (awake and
    alert) child*
  *Suctioning a child with a decreased
    level of consciousness*
  Tracheostomy Tube Suctioning
  *Suctioning a tracheostomy tube*
  Endotracheal Tube Suctioning
  *Suctioning an endotracheal tube*

CHEST PHYSIOTHERAPY/
POSTURAL DRAINAGE
  Percussion
  Vibration
  *Performing chest physiotherapy*

PLACEMENT OF ECG ELECTRODES
  Chest Leads
  Limb Electrodes

**SAFETY PRECAUTIONS**

- "Oxygen in Use" signs should be posted at the child's doorway and at the bedside.
- Make sure that matches and lighters are not used in the area.
- Use only hospital-approved electrical equipment.
- Do not use flammable or volatile solutions in the child's room.

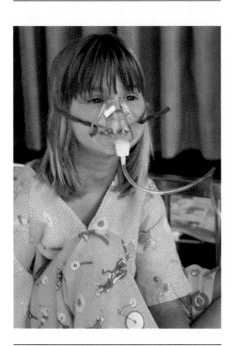

FIGURE 43. Simple face mask.

# ▶ ADMINISTRATION OF OXYGEN

When administering oxygen, the concentration ordered and the age of the child are important. To assess the child's response to the therapy, monitor heart rate, respiratory rate and effort, color, pulse oximeter readings, and level of consciousness.

Humidification is often necessary to prevent nasal passages from drying out. This is provided by attaching a sterile water–filled container to the oxygen or flowmeter with a connecting tube.

Because oxygen is combustible, certain precautions must be taken during its use (see box).

## DELIVERY SYSTEMS

### Masks

The size of the mask is important when administering oxygen. The mask should extend from the bridge of the nose to the cleft of the chin. It should fit snugly on the face but put no pressure on the eyes to avoid stimulating a vagal response.

The following types of masks are available:

- The *simple face mask* (Fig. 43) can deliver from 30–60% oxygen when a flow rate of 6–10 L/min is used.
- The *nonrebreather mask* has a reservoir bag attached to deliver higher concentrations of oxygen, up to 95% with a flow of 10–12 L/min, when a tight seal is maintained.

## Nasal Cannula

A nasal cannula is used to deliver low-flow, low-concentration oxygen. It does not provide humidified oxygen. A flow rate set higher than 6 L/min will irritate the nasopharynx without appreciably improving the child's oxygenation.

The prongs of the cannula are placed in the anterior nares, and the elastic band is placed around the child's head (Fig. 44). Infants, preschool, and school-age children usually tolerate the cannula. Toddlers will usually pull the cannula off their face. A face mask or blow-by tubing is often a more appropriate method of oxygen administration for this age group.

## Tent

An oxygen tent (Fig. 45), in theory, allows for delivery of 50% humidified oxygen, but in practice only 30% humidified oxygen can be achieved. Concentration should be determined with an oxygen analyzer. To avoid air leakage, secure the edges of the tent with blankets.

Access to and visual assessment of the child are difficult when an oxygen tent is used. The child may feel confined, isolated from his or her parents, or claustrophobic when in the tent. The child may respond more favorably to using the mask when awake and the tent while asleep.

## Blow-by Cannula

A blow-by cannula may be either a narrow oxygen catheter with small perforations through which oxygen can flow or corrugated oxygen tubing. This device is used when the child will not tolerate other means of oxygen therapy and when low oxygen concentrations with humidification are needed. The parent can hold the child in his or her lap and direct the tubing toward the child's face, moving it as the child moves. This technique reduces the child's anxiety and facilitates parental involvement in care.

In the ICU the blow-by method can be used for young infants (Fig. 46).

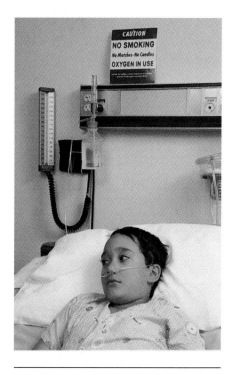

FIGURE 44. Nasal cannula.

FIGURE 45. Oxygen tent.

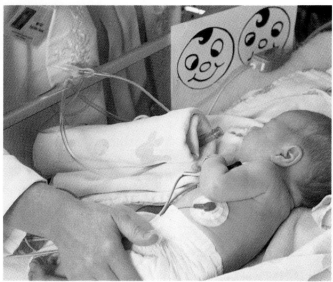

FIGURE 46. Blow-by cannula.

**FIGURE 47.** Oropharyngeal airway of various sizes, each with flange, bite block, curved body.

## ► OROPHARYNGEAL AIRWAY

The oropharyngeal airway is commonly used to maintain an airway in children who are unconscious. It is made of plastic and consists of three parts: a flange, a small bite block, and a curved body (Fig. 47).

This type of airway is designed to keep the tongue of an unconscious child from falling into the posterior pharynx. It is ***never*** used for a conscious infant or child because its insertion might stimulate the gag reflex or vomiting.

Pediatric sizes range from 4 to 10 cm (1½–4 in.) in length. It is important that the airway be the correct size. If it is too large, it can obstruct the larynx. If it is too small, it will push the tongue into the posterior pharynx, causing it to obstruct the airway. The proper size can be estimated by placing the airway alongside the child's face with the bite block parallel to the hard palate and the flange at the level of the central incisors. The distal end of the airway should reach the angle of the jaw (Fig. 48).

**FIGURE 48.** Estimating the size of an oropharyngeal airway.

An oropharyngeal airway is usually inserted by the physician. The child should be assessed closely during the procedure and suction should be available. Once the airway is in place, the child's head and jaw must be maintained in a neutral position.

## ► NASOPHARYNGEAL AIRWAY

The nasopharyngeal airway provides a passage for air between the tongue and the posterior pharyngeal wall. It is used for a conscious child.

This type of airway is made of soft plastic or rubber and comes in various sizes. The length of the tube is determined by measuring the distance from the tip of the nose to the tragus of the ear (Fig. 49). The width must allow for passage through the nares.

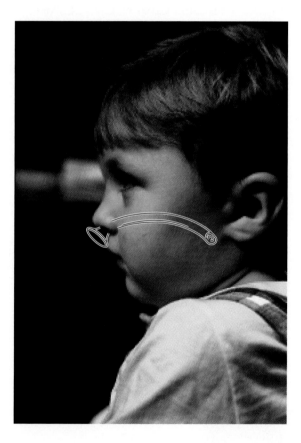

**FIGURE 49.** Estimating the size of a nasopharyngeal airway.

The tip of the airway should be lubricated with a water-soluble gel and inserted into the nares in a posterior direction. During insertion, observe for bleeding, which may exacerbate the obstruction and further compromise airway management.

## ► TRACHEOSTOMY

A tracheostomy is a surgical procedure in which an opening is made in the trachea to create an airway. It can be performed as an acute life-saving procedure or for management of the child with a chronic disease.

Observe the child with a tracheostomy carefully. Vital signs and respiratory status, including breath sounds, respiratory effort, and airway patency should be routinely checked. Be alert for changes in heart or respiratory rate, blood pressure, color, or level of consciousness.

A neonatal or pediatric tracheostomy tube is made of plastic and has an obturator used for insertion only. The tube is held in place with twill tape tied around the child's neck.

A resuscitation bag, oxygen, and suctioning equipment must be kept at the bedside. Have two prepared tracheostomy tubes ready, one that is the size of the child's current tube and one that is the next size smaller, in case of accidental dislodgment. (See the procedure for tracheostomy care later in this discussion.)

## TRACHEOSTOMY COLLAR

The child usually wears a tracheostomy collar (Fig. 50) ("mist collar") at the stoma site to keep the airway warm and moist. The collar may emit either oxygen or room air, depending on the physician's orders. Watch for condensation in the oxygen tubing and empty it regularly; otherwise, the fluid may drip into the tracheostomy tube, causing the child to aspirate.

When the child is in a crib, put the tubing through, rather than over, the bars to prevent fluid from entering the tracheostomy.

## TRACHEOSTOMY CARE

Tracheostomy care is usually performed once per shift. An assistant should **always** be present while tracheostomy care is being performed.

### CLINICAL TIP

*Always* keep a sterile, packaged tracheostomy tube taped to the child's bed so that if the tube dislodges, a new one is available for immediate reintubation.

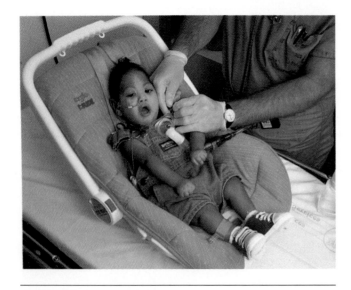

**FIGURE 50.** Infant with a tracheostomy collar.

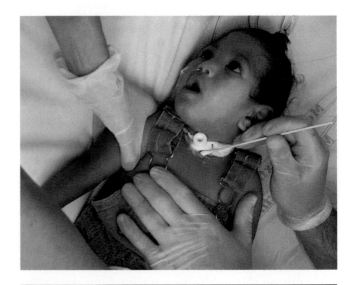

**FIGURE 51.** Cleaning the tracheostomy tube.

## PERFORMING TRACHEOSTOMY CARE

### Preparation

Have an assistant stand on the opposite side of the bed. Put a towel roll under the child's neck to hyperextend the head.

### Selected Equipment

Towel roll
Precut twill tape
Cotton-tipped applicators saturated with half-strength hydrogen peroxide
Cotton-tipped applicators saturated with normal saline
Gauze pads (some moistened with saline and others dry)
Scissors
Tracheal cleaning tray with sterile bowls, pipe cleaners, brush, notched gauze pad
Sterile hydrogen peroxide and sterile normal saline
Suction tray and catheters (see the separate suctioning procedure on p. 101)
*Note:* Equipment is usually available in a prepackaged kit. Prepared tracheostomy tubes, oxygen, resuscitation bag, and suction tray with catheters should be at the bedside.

### Procedure—*Sterile Gloves, Gown, Mask, Goggles*

- Don the sterile gloves.
- Pour sterile normal saline into a sterile bowl and hydrogen peroxide into another bowl.
- Unlock the inner cannula and place it into the bowl containing the hydrogen peroxide.
- Clean the cannula thoroughly with pipe cleaners and rinse in normal saline.
- Replace the inner cannula and lock it into place.
- Using cotton-tipped applicators saturated with half-strength hydrogen peroxide, clean under the tracheostomy tube at the stoma site (Fig. 51). Rinse the stoma with saline applicators. Wash the area behind the flanges of the tracheostomy and around the neck with damp gauze, observing for redness or skin breakdown. Dry thoroughly.
- Hold the tube while your assistant performs the same care on the opposite side.
- Place a notched gauze pad under the stoma.
- With the tube held in place, tie the tape. The best fit is achieved when the child's neck is slightly flexed. The tape should be tied tightly enough to prevent dislodgment but should still be loose enough so that you can fit one finger between it and the child's neck. To make new ties, use two pieces of twill tape. Fold one end of each piece over lengthwise for approximately 1–1½ inches (2.5–4 cm). Cut a small hole in the folded end.

- Have your assistant hold the tube in place. Remove the present tape from the flange.
- Attach the twill tape to the flange by first threading the end with the slit through the hole. Place the distal end of the twill tape through the slit and pull it securely.
- Have your assistant repeat this step on the opposite side.
- Double-knot or triple-knot the tape for security. Do not place the knot at the back of the child's neck, since this might cause the skin to break down when the child is supine.

## ▶ ENDOTRACHEAL TUBE

Endotracheal (ET) tubes are sterile, disposable, and made of a translucent plastic or other synthetic material. The distal end is tapered and has an opening in the side wall (Murphy's eye). The length of the tube is marked in centimeters to serve as a measurement reference point once it is in place. Intubation is usually performed by the physician to protect or maintain the child's airway.

The tubes come in various sizes, both with and without cuffs (Fig. 52). The uncuffed tube is recommended for the child younger than 8–9 years old, since the airway is narrowest at the cricoid ring, sealing the airway effectively without a cuff.

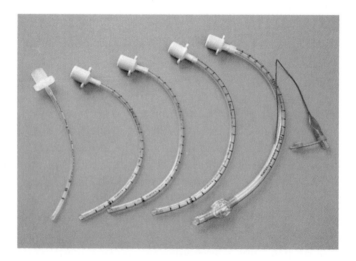

FIGURE 52. Endotracheal tubes.

The size of the tube can be approximated by comparing it with the diameter of the child's little finger or nares. The formula used for children older than 2 years of age is:

$$16 + \text{Age in years}/4 = \text{Size of ET tube}$$

A 3.0 or 3.5 ET tube can usually be used in the full-term newborn. A 4.0 ET tube can be used until the child's first birthday.

Once the tube has been placed by the physician, auscultate for equal breath sounds, and check for symmetry of chest movement and condensation in the tube. A $CO_2$ monitor is sometimes used. Auscultate over the abdomen to ensure that the tube is not in the esophagus. Listen at the trachea for air leaks. Once correct tube placement is verified, note the centimeter marking at the lip or tooth line and tape the tube in place.

Continuously assess breath sounds, color, heart rate on the monitor, and pulse oximeter readout.

## ▶ VENTILATOR

Ventilators are used for children who need assistance with breathing. These children may have a chronic condition, such as a neuromuscular disease or persistent lung pathology, or may be acutely ill or injured and need emergency management of ventilation.

To safely provide care for the ventilated child:

- Be familiar with the ventilator and know which settings have been ordered by the physician, including oxygen concentration, humidity, air temperature, pressure, tidal volume, and inspiratory/expiratory ratio and rate. Identify what the alarms mean, and know how to troubleshoot problems.

- Ensure that the child is attached to a cardiorespiratory monitor and pulse oximeter. Always keep a resuscitation bag and mask at the bedside. Oxygen and suction, along with appropriate-size catheters, should also be at hand.

- Measure arterial blood gases within 15 minutes after the child has been placed on the ventilator and thereafter according to the physician's orders. Assess vital signs every hour, including heart and respiratory rates, blood pressure, temperature, and pulse oximeter reading. Auscultate the lungs in all fields to assess for equal breath sounds. Ensure that the child's respiratory rate is consistent with the ventilator setting.

- Suction the ET tube as necessary. Disconnect the ventilator, oxygenate the child once or twice with a resuscitation bag, suction no more than 15–10 seconds while counting 1 one thousand, 2 one thousand, 3 one thousand,. . . apply the bag again and reoxygenate, and reconnect the ventilator.

- Protect the ET tube by making sure it is well taped and secure. Support the ventilator tubing to decrease traction on the ET tube by attaching the tubing directly to the bed using a gauze roll and a safety pin. Elbow splints may need to be applied to prevent the child from pulling out the tube. Acutely ill or injured children may need to be chemically paralyzed and sedated while on the ventilator. If the child has been given paralytics, watch for signs that further sedation may be needed (eg, a rise in heart rate and blood pressure or tearing).

- Listen and look for air leaks. Make sure that the ventilator is firmly attached to the ET tube.

- Check the reservoir for humidification at least every 8 hours. Refill or replace water as needed. Watch for condensation in the tubing and empty it regularly; otherwise the fluid may drip into the ET tube, causing the child to aspirate.

- Insert a nasogastric or orogastric tube to keep the child's abdomen decompressed. Check its placement.

- Tell the child what you are planning to do; for example, "I'm going to wash your face" or "I'm going to move your arms and legs." The child who is sedated or unresponsive may still be able to hear.

- Support the family by answering their questions. Encourage them to communicate with the child. Have them bring in audio tapes of favorite music or of family members speaking to the child.

# ▶ CARDIOPULMONARY RESUSCITATION*

Cardiopulmonary resuscitation (CPR) is basic life support using techniques to maintain airway, breathing, and circulation (the ABCs). Lay people are routinely taught one-person basic life support. Health care professionals should be skilled in both one- and two-person CPR. The following is the sequence of resuscitation interventions designated by the American Heart Association and the American Academy of Pediatrics.

Clean gloves should be worn in the hospital setting and whenever possible in the community during the resuscitation procedure. A pocket mask or bag valve mask is used whenever possible.

## INFANT

### Unresponsiveness

Unresponsiveness can be determined by gently tapping the infant on the abdomen or soles of the feet. If the infant does not respond, begin basic life support (BLS).

Provide BLS for 1 minute *before* activating the emergency medical services.

### Airway Assessment

Make sure that the airway is patent. Oftentimes, if the infant is unconscious, the tongue will slip into the posterior hypopharynx and cause obstruction. The head needs to be maintained in a neutral position to keep the airway clear. The airway can be opened by using one of two maneuvers: head tilt–chin lift, or jaw thrust.

#### *Head Tilt–Chin Lift* (Fig. 53)
Place one hand on the infant's forehead to gently tilt the head back into a neutral position. *Do not* hyperextend the neck. Place the fingers of your other hand on the bony prominence of the chin and lift the jaw upward and outward.

#### *Jaw Thrust* (Fig. 54)
Standing behind the child's head, place two or three fingers under each side of the jaw at its angle. Lift the jaw upward and outward. This maneuver

---

*Based on Pediatric Basic Life Support. (1992). *Journal of the American Medical Association, 268*(16), 2251–2261; and American Heart Association. (1994). *Pediatric basic life support.* Dallas: Author.

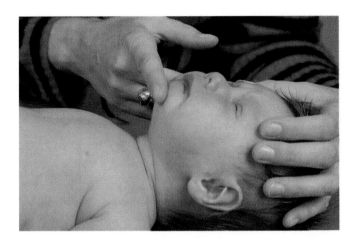

FIGURE 53. Head tilt–chin lift maneuver.

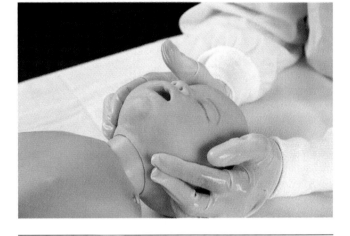

FIGURE 54. Jaw thrust maneuver.

is performed on all children suspected of having cervical spine injury. One person performs CPR while another maintains the jaw thrust position.

## Breathing Assessment

After the airway has been opened, determine whether the infant is breathing (Fig. 55). Check for the rise and fall of the chest and abdomen, and listen and feel for the flow of expelled air at the mouth.

If no spontaneous breathing is detected, begin rescue breathing, maintaining airway patency by using the head tilt–chin lift or the jaw thrust maneuver.

### Mouth-to-Mouth-and-Nose Resuscitation

Take a deep breath. Place your mouth over the nose and mouth of the infant to create a tight seal. Give two slow breaths, each lasting 1–1½ seconds (Fig 56). After giving the first breath, pause to take a breath to maximize the oxygen content that you can deliver.

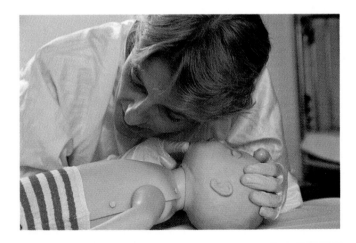

FIGURE 55. Assessing breathing.

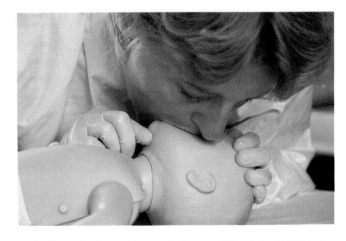

FIGURE 56. Mouth-to-mouth-and-nose resuscitation.

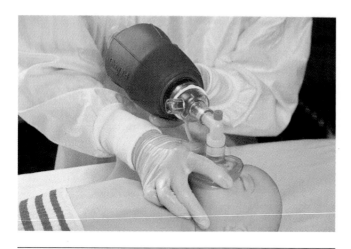

FIGURE 57. Bag and mask resuscitation.

FIGURE 58. Checking for the brachial pulse.

### Bag and Mask Resuscitation (Fig. 57)

The mask should extend from the bridge of the nose to the cleft of the chin, and should not cover the eyes. A tight seal must be maintained. The bag, with an attached reservoir and hooked up to 100% oxygen, must be the proper size for the infant, usually between 250 mL for the newborn and 500 mL for the older infant. Two breaths are given initially.

### Special Considerations

The volume of air, delivered either by mouth-to-mouth or bag and mask resuscitation, should be just enough to produce a visible chest rise. If the chest does not rise, the airway may no longer be patent. The position of the head should be readjusted or the breath volume increased.

Remember that gastric distention can occur with either mouth-to-mouth or bag and mask rescue breathing. This distention compromises ventilation by elevating the diaphragm and decreasing lung size. It may also stimulate vomiting.

## Circulation

Once the airway has been opened and two breaths have been given, assess circulation by checking for a brachial pulse (Fig. 58). The brachial pulse lies on the inside of the upper arm, between the shoulder and the elbow. Assess for 10 seconds before determining pulselessness. If a pulse is palpated, perform rescue breathing every 3 seconds (20 times per minute). If no pulse is felt, begin chest compressions, delivering ventilations between every 5 compressions (Fig. 59).

Position the infant on a hard surface, with the head in a neutral position to ensure airway patency. (The rescuer may hold the infant, using one arm as the surface.)

- Apply compressions to the lower third of the sternum, which can be located by placing your index finger at the intermammary line and then putting the middle and ring fingers next to it. Keep your other hand on the infant's head to maintain airway patency.

FIGURE 59. Alternating breathing and chest compressions.

- With middle and ring fingers, compress the chest ½–1 inch (1–2.5 cm) (or approximately one third to one half the depth of the chest) at a rate of at least 100 compressions per minute. With the pause for ventilations, this method will equal about 80 compressions per minute. At the end of each compression, allow the chest to return to the normal position before beginning the next compression.
- Rescue breaths and compressions are performed at a ratio of 1:5 with a pause for ventilations for both one- and two-rescuer CPR.
- Reassess the infant after 20 cycles (one "CPR minute"). Palpate the brachial pulse for 5 seconds. If the pulse is absent, continue the cycle for another 3–5 minutes before reassessment.
- If the infant has a pulse but is not breathing, continue rescue breathing at a rate of 20 times per minute (once every 3 seconds).
- If the infant has a return of both pulse and respirations and is *not* a trauma victim, place the infant in the "recovery" (side-lying) position. This position is used to protect the airway.

## CHILD BETWEEN 1 AND 8 YEARS

### Unresponsiveness

Unresponsiveness can be determined by gently tapping the child and speaking loudly enough to get a response. If the child does not respond, begin BLS.

Provide BLS for 1 minute *before* activating the emergency medical services.

### Airway and Breathing Assessment

In general, airway and breathing assessment for the child between 1 and 8 years of age is the same as for the infant (see the earlier discussion).

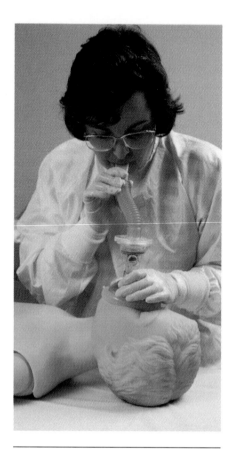

FIGURE 60. Mouth-to-mouth resuscitation using a mask with a one-way valve.

### Mouth-to-Mouth Resuscitation With Mask

Rescue breathing can be performed using a mask with a one-way valve. This method provides an infection-control barrier (Fig. 60).

Place the mask over the child's nose and mouth, creating a tight seal. Take a deep breath. Give two slow breaths, each lasting 1–1½ seconds. After giving the first breath, pause to take a breath to maximize the oxygen content that you are delivering.

### Bag and Mask Resuscitation

The mask should be the correct size, extending from the bridge of the nose to the cleft of the chin, and should not cover the eyes. A tight seal must be maintained. The bag (500 mL for younger children and 1000 mL for school-age children), with an attached reservoir and hooked up to 100% oxygen, must be the proper size for the child. Two breaths are given initially.

### Special Considerations

The volume of air, delivered either by mouth-to-mask or bag and mask resuscitation, should be just enough to produce a visible chest rise. If the chest does not rise, either the airway is no longer patent and the position of the head needs to be readjusted or the breath volume needs to be increased. If mouth-to-mouth breathing is performed, a mechanical barrier should be used and the rescuer's mouth should cover only the mouth of the child.

Remember that gastric distention can occur with either mouth-to-mask or bag and mask rescue breathing. This distention compromises ventilation by elevating the diaphragm and decreasing lung size. It may also stimulate vomiting.

## Circulation

Once the airway has been opened and two breaths have been given, assess circulation by checking for a carotid pulse (Fig. 61). The carotid pulse lies on the side of the neck between the trachea and the sternocleidomastoid muscle. Assess for 10 seconds before determining pulselessness. If a pulse is palpated, perform rescue breathing every 3 seconds (20 times per minute). If no pulse is felt, begin chest compressions, delivering ventilations between every 5 compressions.

Position the child on a hard surface, with the head in a neutral position to ensure airway patency.

- Apply compressions to the lower third of the sternum while positioned at the child's side.
- Using the middle and index fingers of the hand closest to the child's feet, trace the lower margin of the child's ribs to the notch where the ribs and the sternum meet. Place your middle finger on this notch, and put the index finger adjacent to it on the sternum. Place the heel of one hand on the sternum next to the point where the index finger was located (Fig. 62). Make sure to keep your fingers off the chest.
- Using the heel of one hand, compress the chest 1–1½ inches (2.5–4 cm) (approximately one third to one half the depth of the chest) (Fig. 63) at a rate of 100 compressions per minute. With the pause for ventilations, this method will equal about 80 compressions per minute. At

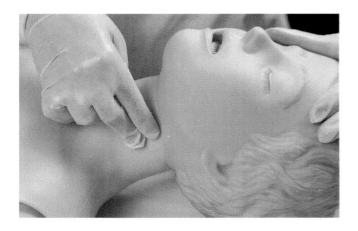

FIGURE 61. Checking for the carotid pulse.

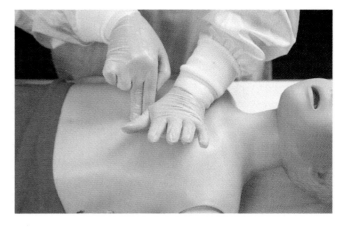

FIGURE 62. Locating the site of chest compressions.

the end of each compression, allow the chest to return to the normal position before beginning the next compression. Maintain the head tilt during this time with your other hand.

- Rescue breaths and compressions are performed at a ratio of 1:5 with a pause for ventilations for both one- and two-rescuer CPR.

- Reassess the child after 20 cycles or one "CPR minute." Palpate the carotid pulse for 5 seconds. If the pulse is absent, continue the cycle for another 3–5 minutes before reassessment.

- If the child has a pulse but is not breathing, continue rescue breathing at a rate of 20 times per minute (once every 3 seconds).

- If the child has a return of both pulse and respirations and is *not* a trauma victim, place the child in the "recovery" (side-lying) position. This position is used to protect the airway.

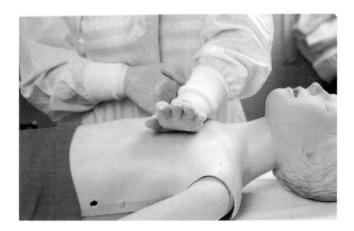

FIGURE 63. Chest compressions.

# ► FOREIGN BODY AIRWAY OBSTRUCTION

Signs and symptoms of airway obstruction may be caused by respiratory disorders (eg, croup or epiglottitis) or a foreign body.

Attempts to clear the airway should be made in the following situations:

1. *For the witnessed or strongly suspected aspiration of a foreign body.* Encourage the child to continue coughing and breathing as long as the cough is forceful. If the cough becomes ineffective and soundless, if increased respiratory difficulty or stridor is noted, or if the victim loses consciousness, the emergency medical services system must be activated and attempts must be made to remove the obstruction.
2. *When the airway remains obstructed during attempts to provide rescue breathing.*

Clean gloves should be worn when attempting to remove a foreign body obstruction.

## INFANT

### Unconscious Infant

- If an infant is found unconscious, begin assessment by using the ABCs. Call aloud "Help!"
- If the infant is not breathing, try to ventilate either by mouth-to-mouth-and-nose resuscitation or with a bag and mask (refer to the CPR guidelines for rescue breathing presented earlier in this unit).
- If the airway is obstructed, reposition the infant's head and attempt to ventilate again.
- If unsuccessful, activate the emergency medical services (EMS) system.
- If the airway is still obstructed, do not check for the pulse. Instead, perform up to 5 back blows (Fig. 64), followed by up to 5 chest thrusts with the fingers in the same position used for CPR (Fig. 65). Then, using a tongue-jaw lift (performed by placing your index finger on the bony prominence of the infant's chin and your thumb in the mouth on the tongue; then pulling up and out to open the mouth), look in the infant's mouth for the foreign body and remove it if seen. *Do not* perform a blind sweep. If no object is found, try to ventilate the infant again. If the obstruction is still present, reposition the infant's head and attempt to ventilate once again.
- If the obstruction remains, begin another series of back blows and chest thrusts. Look in the mouth, try to ventilate, reposition the head, and attempt to ventilate again. Continue with this pattern until the airway is clear.
- Once the airway is clear, give two slow full breaths. Check for a pulse. At this point, provide whatever BLS maneuvers are necessary.

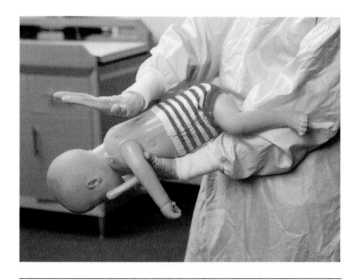

**FIGURE 64.** Back blows.

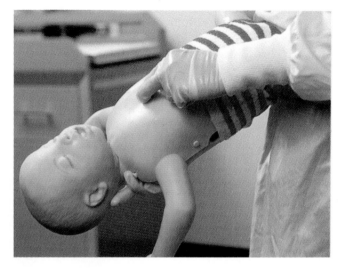

**FIGURE 65.** Chest thrusts.

## CHILD BETWEEN 1 AND 8 YEARS

### Conscious Child

- Abdominal thrusts (Heimlich maneuver) (Fig. 66) can be performed with the child either sitting or standing.
- Stand behind the child, with your arms under the child's axilla and around the chest. Place the thumb of one fist against the abdomen in the midline, below the xiphoid and above the navel. Grasp your fist with your other hand.
- Deliver up to 5 quick upward thrusts. Each thrust should be a distinct effort to remove the obstruction. The series of 5 thrusts should be repeated until the obstruction is cleared or the child becomes unconscious.

**FIGURE 66.** Abdominal thrusts (Heimlich maneuver).

## Unconscious Child

Place the child in a supine position and kneel, straddling the child's body at the hips (see Fig. 67).

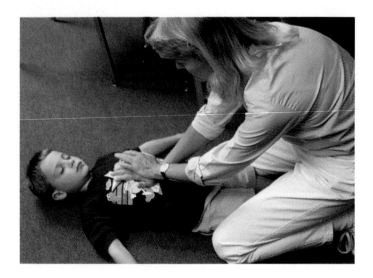

FIGURE 67. Performing abdominal thrusts on an unconscious child.

- Assess for breathing. If the child is not breathing, try to ventilate either by mouth-to-mouth resuscitation or with a bag and mask (refer to the CPR guidelines for rescue breathing presented earlier in this unit). If the airway is obstructed, reposition the child's head and attempt to ventilate again.

- If the airway is still obstructed, do not check for a pulse. Instead, place the heel of your hand on the child's abdomen in the midline, between the xiphoid and navel; then place your other hand over the wrist (Fig. 67). Press into the abdomen, using both hands in quick upward strokes, and deliver up to 5 thrusts. Each thrust should be a distinct attempt to eliminate the obstruction.

- Using the tongue-jaw lift described earlier for the unconscious infant, look into the mouth for a foreign body and remove it if seen. *Do not* perform a blind sweep. If a foreign body is not visualized, open the airway and attempt to ventilate. If the airway is still obstructed, reposition the child's head and attempt to ventilate once again.

- If the obstruction remains, begin another series of abdominal thrusts, look in the mouth, try to ventilate, reposition the head, and attempt to ventilate again. Continue with this pattern until the airway is clear.

- Once the airway is clear, give two slow full breaths. Check for a pulse. At this point, provide whatever BLS maneuvers are necessary.

# ► SUCTIONING

The nose, mouth, tracheostomy tube, or endotracheal tube may require suctioning. It is important to obtain baseline vital signs before and after the procedure. When suctioning, watch for a decrease in pulse rate, an increase or decrease in respiratory rate, or a change in color. Bradycardia may be a sign of vagal stimulation. If any of these signs occur, stop immediately and give the child oxygen using blow-by, a face mask, or a resuscitation bag.

The size of the suction catheter depends on the size, age, and weight of the child or on the tube requiring suctioning. Usually a tonsil-tip or Yankauer catheter is used for oral suctioning when copious, thick secretions need to be removed.

Have an assistant gently restrain the child to keep the child's hands out of the way. The assistant will need to keep the child's head in the midline position. The intubated child is frequently sedated.

## NASAL/ORAL SUCTIONING

The nose and mouth are suctioned when excess secretions are present or when a decreased level of consciousness interferes with the child's ability to clear normal secretions. A bulb syringe is used to remove secretions from an infant's nose or mouth. Care needs to be taken to avoid stimulating the gag reflex. Normal saline nose drops may be used before nasal suction with a bulb syringe to loosen secretions. A catheter is used to remove secretions from an older child's mouth or nose, a tracheostomy tube, or an endotracheal tube. The child with a decreased level of consciousness will likely require deep suctioning to remove secretions.

## USING A BULB SYRINGE

### Procedure—*Clean Gloves*

- Deflate the bulb.
- Insert the tip of the bulb syringe into the infant's naris (Fig. 68).
- Allow the bulb to inflate and remove the syringe from the naris (Fig. 69).
- Expel the secretions into the proper receptacle.
- Repeat as necessary.

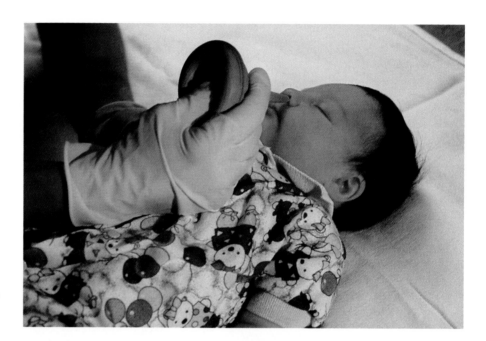

FIGURE 68. Insertion of a deflated bulb syringe.

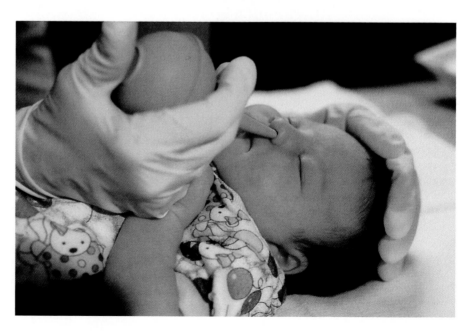

FIGURE 69. Removal of a reinflated bulb syringe.

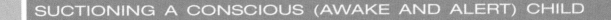

## SUCTIONING A CONSCIOUS (AWAKE AND ALERT) CHILD

### Preparation—*Clean Gloves*

Have an assistant help you maintain the child's head in the midline position. The head of the bed should be raised to 30–45 degrees. Turn on and set the wall suction to the level ordered by the physician or suggested in your facility's procedure manual.

### Selected Equipment

Appropriate-size suction catheter
Sterile container with sterile normal saline
Suction kit
Water-soluble lubricant

### Procedure—*2 Sterile Gloves*

- Keep your dominant hand sterile and your nondominant hand clean for the procedure.
- If possible, encourage the child to cough to make the secretions pool in the hypopharynx.
- Attach the proximal end of the catheter to the wall suction connecting tubing, making sure to keep the distal end sterile.
- Keep your dominant hand sterile to manipulate the catheter.
- Remove the protective sheath from the catheter, and test the suction by placing it in a cup of saline.
- With your dominant hand, insert the suction catheter into the child's naris and suction for no more than 5 to 10 seconds, while gently rotating the catheter. (The depth of insertion depends on the size of the child.)
- Remove and irrigate the catheter with sterile normal saline.
- Repeat as necessary.
- Assess the child for adequacy of oxygenation.

*Note:* The mouth may also be suctioned for secretions, but care needs to be taken to avoid stimulating the gag reflex.

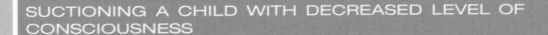

## SUCTIONING A CHILD WITH DECREASED LEVEL OF CONSCIOUSNESS

### Preparation

Depending on the child's level of consciousness, you may need an assistant to help keep the child's head in the midline position. The head of the bed should be raised to 30–45 degrees. Turn on and set the wall suction to the level ordered by the physician or suggested in your facility's procedure manual.

## Selected Equipment

Appropriate-size suction catheter
Sterile container with sterile normal saline
Oxygen
Bag-valve-mask

## Procedure—*2 Sterile Gloves*

- Place an oxygen mask on the child's face.
- If possible, encourage the child to cough to make the secretions pool in the hypopharynx.
- Attach the proximal end of the catheter to the wall suction connecting tubing, making sure to keep the distal end sterile.
- Keep your dominant hand sterile and your nondominant hand clean for the procedure. Use only the dominant hand to manipulate the catheter.
- Remove the protective sheath from the catheter, and test the suction by placing it in a cup of saline.
- Remove the child's oxygen mask.

### Nasal/Oral Suctioning

- With your dominant hand, insert the catheter into the child's naris or mouth without occluding the suction port.
- Slowly advance the catheter only into the hypopharynx.
- Rotate the catheter, applying intermittent suction for 5–10 seconds.
- Remove the catheter and clear the tubing with sterile saline. Repeat as necessary.
- Assess the child for adequacy of oxygention.

### Deep Suctioning

- With your dominant hand, insert the catheter beyond the hypopharynx and into the trachea (the length advanced is determined by the size of the child). *Do not* occlude the suction port.
- When the catheter is in place, gently rotate it while suctioning intermittently. To prevent hypoxia, *do not* suction for more than 5–10 seconds.
- Allow the child to breath normally, and give supplemental oxygen between suctionings.
- Remove the catheter and clear the tubing with sterile saline. Repeat as necessary.

# TRACHEOSTOMY TUBE SUCTIONING

A tracheostomy is an opening through the neck directly into the trachea. It is used to provide adequate ventilation when the child is unable to breathe effectively alone. This is a surgical opening and must be treated carefully to maintain patency, ensure freedom from infection, and promote adequate oxygenation.

## SUCTIONING A TRACHEOSTOMY TUBE

## Preparation

- Place the head of the bed at a 30 degree angle.
- Turn on and set the wall suction to the level ordered by the physician or suggested in your facility's procedure manual. Turn on the oxygen source attached to the resuscitation bag to inflate the reservoir bag so it is ready to use.

## Selected Equipment

Have the following equipment at the bedside: additional prepared tracheostomy tubes (see the description under tracheostomy care, earlier), resuscitation bag with attached oxygen source, and suction.
Appropriate-size suction catheter
Sterile container with sterile normal saline

## Procedure—*2 Sterile Gloves*

- Keep your dominant hand sterile and your nondominant hand clean for the procedure. Use only the dominant hand to manipulate the catheter.
- With your dominant hand, remove the catheter from the paper sheath, keeping it sterile.
- With your nondominant hand, connect the proximal end of the catheter to the wall suction connecting tubing.
- Place the distal end of the catheter in a cup of sterile saline to test the suction.
- With your nondominant hand, remove the humidity source from the child's tracheostomy tube. Oxygenate the child before suctioning, using a resuscitation bag in your nondominant hand. Give several breaths.

- Remove the resuscitation bag.
- Using your dominant hand, place the suction catheter into the tube, making sure no suction is being applied at this time. Advance the catheter no farther than 0.5 cm (¼ in.) below the edge of the tracheostomy tube.
- Once the catheter is in place, intermittently cover the suction port and rotate the catheter (Fig. 70).

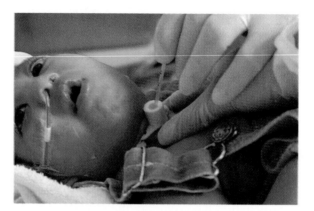

**FIGURE 70.** Tracheostomy tube suctioning.

- Remove the catheter and irrigate it in a cup of sterile saline. To prevent the child from becoming hypoxic, *do not* suction for longer than 5–10 seconds.
- Repeat as necessary, oxygenating between suctionings.
- Alternately, two people can do the procedure with one applying the resuscitation bag and the other performing suction.

# ENDOTRACHEAL TUBE SUCTIONING

Use extreme care when handling the endotracheal (ET) tube during procedures such as suctioning to avoid dislodging the tube unintentionally. Hold the tube firmly in place while the ventilator is being disconnected, when the resuscitation bag is being attached and removed, during hyperventilation, and during suctioning.

## SUCTIONING AN ENDOTRACHEAL TUBE

## Preparation

Turn on and set the wall suction to the level ordered by the physician or suggested in your facility's procedure manual. Turn on the oxygen source attached to the resuscitation bag to inflate the reservoir bag so it is ready for use.

## Selected Equipment

Appropriate-size suction catheter
Sterile container with sterile normal saline

## Procedure—*2 Sterile Gloves*

- Keep your dominant hand sterile and your nondominant hand clean for the procedure. Use only the dominant hand to manipulate the catheter.
- With your dominant hand, remove the catheter from the paper sheath, keeping it sterile.
- With your nondominant hand, connect the proximal end of the catheter to the wall suction connecting tubing. Place the distal end of the catheter in a cup of sterile saline to test the suction pressure.
- If the child is being ventilated, have an assistant disconnect the ventilator and manually oxygenate the child before suctioning. Give several breaths.
- Remove the resuscitation bag.
- With your dominant hand, place the suction catheter into the ET tube, making sure that no suction is being applied at this time. Advance the catheter no farther than 0.5 cm (¼ in.) below the edge of the ET tube. Before inserting the catheter, determine how far the suction catheter can be advanced by making a visual comparison of the airway and the ET tube length.
- Once the catheter is in place, intermittently cover the suction port and rotate the catheter.
- Remove the catheter and irrigate it in a cup of sterile saline. To prevent the child from becoming hypoxic, *do not* suction for longer than 5–10 seconds.
- Repeat as necessary, oxygenating the child between suctionings.

## ► CHEST PHYSIOTHERAPY/POSTURAL DRAINAGE

In postural drainage, positioning is used to take advantage of gravity in the drainage of secretions. Specific lung areas are drained by gravity, with mucus moving from the affected bronchioles into the bronchi and trachea.

The drainage procedures are usually done before the morning meal, and again at bedtime if the child is subject to nighttime mucus retention, plugging of airways, and/or coughing. With certain conditions, such as cystic fibrosis, drainage is often done before each meal and before bedtime. Bronchodilators are frequently administered by a hand-held nebulizer, intermittent positive pressure breathing (IPPB), or a metered-dose aerosol before drainage is performed.

Chest physiotherapy is important for children who have excessive sputum production or retained bronchial secretions. During postural drainage, two maneuvers can be done to aid in drainage: percussion and vibration (Fig. 71A, 71B, and 71C).

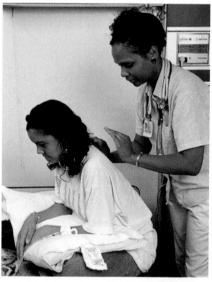
A

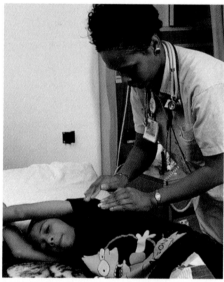
B

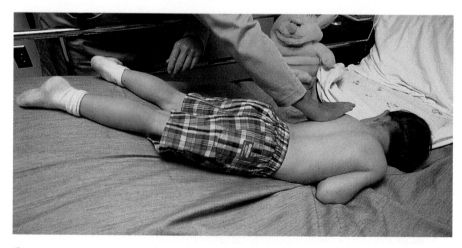
C

FIGURE 71. **A** and **B,** Postural drainage can be achieved by clapping with a cupped hand on the chest wall over the segment to be drained to create vibrations that are transmitted to the bronchi to dislodge secretions. Various positions are used, depending on the location of the obstruction (see Table 8). **C,** Vibration technique.

## PERCUSSION

Percussion is performed by clapping the chest wall with cupped hands. This action produces chest vibrations that dislodge retained secretions.

- Cup your hands, holding your fingers together so that the contour of your cupped hand conforms with the chest wall. Keep your wrists loose and flexible, and clap the area with the palm of your hand. Listen for a hollow sound. Alternate hands, clapping the area in a rhythmic pattern for 3–5 minutes.
- Alternatively, you can use a round oxygen mask, a rubber baby bottle nipple (use only for infants), or a manufactured percussor.
- Encourage the child to take a deep breath and to cough after percussion.

## VIBRATION

Vibration is the application of a downward vibrating pressure with the flat part of the palm over the area that is being drained (Fig. 71C). This maneuver is done only during exhalation.

- Tell the child to take deep breaths, inhaling through the nose and exhaling through the mouth.
- Place one of your hands on top of the other on the designated area, keeping your arms and shoulders straight. Vibrate the area by tensing and relaxing your arms for 10–15 seconds. Perform these tensing/relaxing actions for 10–15 minutes.
- Encourage coughing between vibrations.

After completion, reassess the child's vital signs and respiratory status, noting any changes.

## PERFORMING CHEST PHYSIOTHERAPY

### Preparation

Perform a baseline respiratory assessment.

### Procedure

#### Child

- Place the child in the recommended position and maintain that position for 10–15 minutes. (The positions used for each patient are based on the location of mucus obstruction. In generalized obstructive lung disease, the lower lobes are drained first, followed by the middle lobes and lingula, and the upper lobes are drained last. The various positions used for bronchial drainage in a child are described in Table 8).
- Encourage the child to cough up any sputum.
- Return the child to a normal position.

**8** Positions Used for Postural Drainage of the Child

### Bronchopulmonary segments

| Location | No. | Color key |
|---|---|---|
| **Right Upper Lobe** | | |
| Apical | 1 | Red ▲ |
| Anterior | 2 | Light blue ▲ |
| Posterior | 3 | Green ▲ |
| **Right Middle Lobe** | | |
| Lateral | 4 | Purple ▲ |
| Medial | 5 | Orange ▲ |
| **Right Lower Lobe** | | |
| Superior | 6 | Lavender ▲ |
| Medial basal | 7 | Olive ▲ |
| Anterior basal | 8 | Yellow ▲ |
| Lateral basal | 9 | Red ▲ |
| Posterior basal | 10 | Turquoise ▲ |
| **Left Upper Lobe** | | |
| Upper apical— posterior | 1 | Red ▲ |
| Anterior | 2 | Light blue ▲ |
| Lower—lingular | | |
| Superior | 4 | Purple ▲ |
| Inferior | 5 | Orange ▲ |
| **Left Lower Lobe** | | |
| Superior | 6 | Lavender ▲ |
| Anteromedial | 8 | Yellow ▲ |
| Lateral basal | 9 | Red ▲ |
| Posterior basal | 10 | Turquoise ▲ |

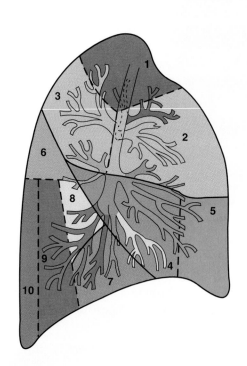

## Lower Lobes

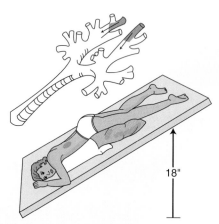

▲ *Posterior Basal Segment (10)*
Elevate foot of table or bed 18 inches or 30 degrees. Have child lie prone, head down, with pillow under hips. Upper leg can be flexed over a pillow for support. (Percuss over lower ribs close to spine on each side of chest.)

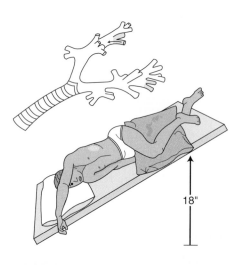

▲ *Lateral Basal Segment (9)*
Elevate foot of table or bed 18 inches or 30 degrees. Have child lie prone, then rotate ¼ turn upward. Upper leg can be flexed over a pillow for support. (Percuss over uppermost portion of lower ribs.)

▲ *Anterior Basal Segment (8)*
Elevate foot of table or bed 18 inches or 30 degrees. Have child lie on side, head down, pillow under knees. (Percuss over lower ribs just beneath axilla.)

**8** Positions Used for Postural Drainage of the Child (continued)

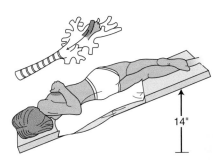

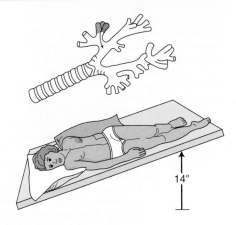

**Lower Lobes—cont'd**

▲ *Superior Segment (6)*
Place bed or table flat. Have child lie with pillows under hips. (Percuss over middle of back below tip of scapula on either side of spine.)

**Right Middle Lobe**

▲ *Lateral Segment (4)*
▲ *Medial Segment (5)*
Elevate foot of table or bed 14 inches or about 15 degrees. Have child lie head down on left side and rotate ¼ turn backward. Pillow may be placed behind child from shoulder to hip. Knees should be flexed. (Percuss over right nipple area.)

**Left Upper Lobe**

▲ *Lingular Segment—Superior (4)*
▲ *Inferior (4)*
Elevate foot of table or bed 14 inches or about 15 degrees. Have child lie head down on right side and rotate ¼ turn backward. Pillow may be placed behind child from shoulder to hip. Knees should be flexed. (Percuss over left nipple area.)

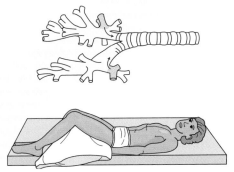

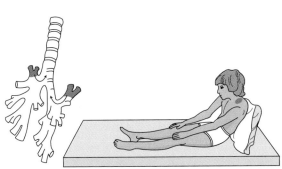

**Upper Lobes**

▲ *Posterior Segment (3)*
Have child sit up and lean over folded pillow at 30 degree angle. (Percuss over upper back on each side of chest.)

▲ *Anterior Segment (2)*
Place bed or drainage table flat. Have child lie supine with pillow under knees. (Percuss between clavicle and nipple on each side of chest.)

▲ *Apical Segment (1)*
Place bed or drainage table flat. Have child lean back on pillow at 30 degree angle. (Percuss over area between clavicle and top of scapula on each side of chest.)

*Modified from material provided by Datalizer Slide Charts, Addison, IL.*

## PERFORMING CHEST PHYSIOTHERAPY (cont.)

### Infant
- Use the following positions to facilitate bronchial drainage:

## Lower Lobes

### Posterior Basal Segment
- Place the infant prone on a pillow on your lap.
- Percuss and vibrate the back at the lower ribs.

### Lateral Basal Segment
- Place the infant prone on a pillow on your lap at a 30 degree angle.
- Rotate the infant's body slightly so that one side is elevated.
- Percuss and vibrate over the lower ribs.
- Turn and repeat.

### Anterior Basal Segment
- Extend your legs and keep them slightly flexed (use a chair for support).
- Place the infant, supported on a pillow, in a side-lying position (30 degree angle) with the head down.
- Percuss and vibrate the area over the ribs under the axilla.
- Turn and repeat.

### Superior Segment
- Place the infant prone on a pillow on your lap.
- Percuss and vibrate the back.

## Upper Lobes

### Lateral and Medial Segments
- Place the infant on your lap in the prone position.
- Rotate the infant slightly so that the right side is elevated.
- Percuss and vibrate the anterior chest at the nipple.
- Turn the infant and repeat.

### Posterior Segment
- Place the infant on your lap in a sitting position and leaning forward on a pillow at about a 30 degree angle.
- Percuss and vibrate both sides of the upper back.

### Anterior Segment
- Place the infant supine on your lap.
- Percuss and vibrate the area between the clavicle and the midchest at the nipple line.

### Apical Segment
- Place the infant on your lap in a sitting position. Lower the infant to a 30 degree reclining position, using a pillow for support.
- Percuss and vibrate the area between the clavicles and the scapulae.

# ► PLACEMENT OF ECG ELECTRODES

The electrocardiogram (ECG) is a graphic representation of the electricity produced by the heart muscle. The equipment needed is an ECG recorder and patches (or suction cups with conductive gel). Following cleaning of the sites with alcohol swabs, electrodes are placed both on the chest and limbs in the following manner.

## CHEST LEADS

$V_1$—4th intercostal space to right of sternum

$V_2$—4th intercostal space to left of sternum

$V_3$—midway between $V_2$ and $V_4$

$V_4$—5th left intercostal space at midclavicular line

$V_5$—5th left intercostal space at anterior axillary line (midway between $V_4$ and $V_6$)

$V_6$—5th left intercostal space at midaxillary line

## LIMB ELECTRODES

Electrodes are placed on the upper extremities slightly above the wrists and on the lower extremities just above the ankles.

# NUTRITION 10

## ► GASTRIC TUBES

Gastric tubes are used in infants and children to provide a means of alimentation and to decompress or empty the stomach. The size of the nasogastric or orogastric tube is determined by the age, size, and weight of the child.

### OROGASTRIC TUBES

Orogastric tubes are used in newborns and young infants who are obligate nose breathers, and in older children who are unconscious, unresponsive, or intubated.

## INSERTING AND REMOVING AN OROGASTRIC TUBE

### Preparation

- Place the child supine with the head of the bed elevated, unless contraindicated.
- Use the tube to measure the distance from the mouth to the tragus of the ear and then to the xiphoid process to determine the distance to the stomach. (Alternatively, use a point midway between the xiphoid and the umbilicus.) Mark the tube with tape.

### Selected Equipment

Appropriate-size orogastric tube
Suction catheter
Water-soluble lubricant
Stethoscope
20-mL syringe to check tube placement

### Procedure—*Clean Gloves*

#### Insertion

- Have suction at hand. Apply a water-soluble lubricant to the tube.
- Position the child with the neck slightly hyperextended. Open the child's mouth and insert the tube toward the back of the throat. Continue advancing the tube slowly until you reach the mark.
- Check the tube for placement by aspirating the stomach contents and checking the pH; a pH of 3 or below indicates stomach placement. An alternate method of checking placement is to auscultate over the abdomen while a small amount of air (5 mL or up to 10 mL for an older child) is injected through the tube into the stomach. Sometimes an x-ray is used to verify correct placement. Assess the child's respiratory status and color. A change in either may indicate that the tube is located in the trachea rather than in the esophagus.
- Once you are assured that the tube is in place, tape it securely to one side of the child's mouth. Place two pieces of tape in a V pattern around the tube at the lip. If necessary, use a third piece of tape over the other two. Clamp the end of the tube if it is not being used for feeding or suctioning.

#### Removal

- Have suction available.
- Instill approximately 10–20 mL of air into the tube to remove any secretions.
- Untape the tube, pinch or fold it to prevent fluid leakage, and gently withdraw it.

## NASOGASTRIC TUBES

Nasogastric tubes are used more frequently than orogastric tubes. They are inserted to provide alimentation, to decompress the stomach, or to empty the stomach of its contents in preparation for surgery or lavage.

## INSERTING AND REMOVING A NASOGASTRIC TUBE

### Preparation

- Tell the preschool-age child what will happen in very simple terms. Give the school-age child and adolescent a rationale for the procedure. Since placement of the tube is uncomfortable, allow the child to express his or her feelings and seek the support of family members.
- Place the child supine, with the head of the bed elevated to the high Fowler's position, if possible. Restrain younger children because they will fight against the insertion of the tube. An assistant can hold the child's body and arms with his or her body, or the child can be put in a modified mummy restraint. The child's head will need to be held in the midline position.
- Use the tube to measure the distance from the tip of the nose to the tragus of the ear and then to the xiphoid process to determine the distance to the stomach (Fig. 72). (Alternatively, use a point midway between the xiphoid and the umbilicus.) Mark the tube at the correct length with tape.

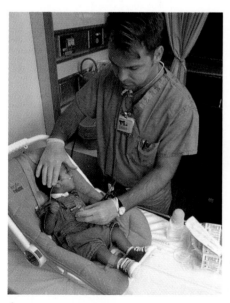
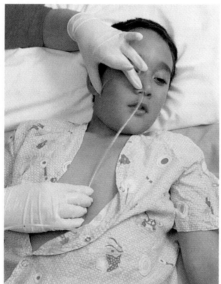

A                                    B

FIGURE 72. Measuring for nasogastric tube placement in **A**, infant, and **B**, child. (A similar technique is used in measuring for orogastric tube insertion. See the previous discussion.)

## Selected Equipment

Appropriate-size nasogastric tube
Suction catheter
Water-soluble lubricant
Stethoscope
20-mL syringe to check tube placement

### Procedure—*Clean Gloves*

### *Insertion*

- Have suction at hand. Apply water-soluble lubricant to the distal end of the tube.
- With the child's neck slightly hyperextended, insert the tube into the child's naris, gently advancing it straight back along the floor of the nasal passages. If resistance is felt at the curve of the nasopharynx, use slight pressure or rotate the tube to continue advancing it.
- If the child gags when the tube reaches beyond the oropharynx, flex the child's neck. If the child can take fluids by mouth, have him or her sip water through a straw and swallow it to ease the passage of the tube over the glottis. If the child is not allowed anything by mouth, have him or her swallow.
- After the gag reflex is suppressed, continue advancing the tube slowly until you reach the mark.
- Check the tube for placement by aspirating the stomach contents and checking the pH; a pH of 3 or under indicates placement in the stomach. An alternate method of checking placement is to auscultate over the abdomen while a small amount of air (5 mL or up to 10 mL for older children) is injected through the tube into the stomach (Fig. 73). Sometimes an x-ray is used to verify correct placement. Assess the child's respiratory status and color. A change in either may indicate that the tube is located in the trachea rather than in the esophagus.

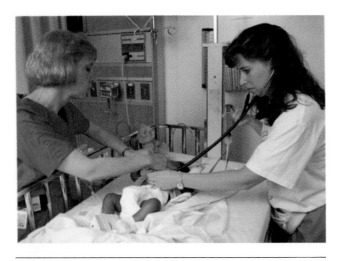

**FIGURE 73.** Checking for nasogastric tube placement.

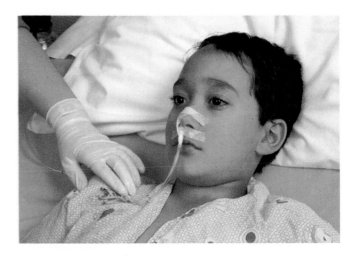

**FIGURE 74.** Nasogastric tube taped securely in place.

- Once you are assured that the tube is in place, tape it securely by placing two pieces of tape in a V pattern around the tube and attaching it to the nose or cheek (Fig. 74). If necessary, use a second piece of tape over the first.

## *Removal*

- Have suction available.
- Place the child in a Fowler's position.
- Instill approximately 10–15 mL of air into the tube to remove any secretions.
- Unfasten the tape, ask the child to hold his or her breath, pinch the tube, and gently pull it out.

## GASTROSTOMY TUBES

Gastrostomy tubes are surgically placed in the stomach and are used primarily for gavage feeding. The tube should remain clamped when it is not being used for feeding or decompression.

Observe the site for skin breakdown. Keep the area clean and dry. Place a clean dry dressing over the site at every shift. A 2 × 2 or 4 × 4 inch gauze pad can be used. A diagonal cut is made halfway into the square and placed around the tube with tape used at the edges to secure it.

Keep the tube as immobile as possible to prevent unintentional removal or displacement. Tube placement can be checked by aspirating a small amount of gastric contents before each feeding.

The gastrostomy feeding button is a flexible silicone device that is often used for children who require long-term enteral feedings.

## ▶ GAVAGE FEEDING

Infants and children require gavage, or tube feeding, to counteract absorption disorders, to provide supplemental feedings, and to conserve calories for growth. Feedings can be either continuous or bolus. They can be administered by gravity (Fig. 75) or by pump. A pump is preferred because it permits better regulation of the rate and volume of the feeding. See Table 15–1 in Ball and Bindler's *Pediatric Nursing* for care of gastrostomy tubes and administration of feedings.

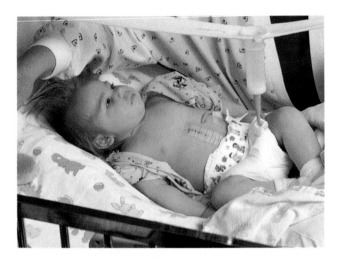

**FIGURE 75.** Gavage feeding by gravity.

## ADMINISTERING A GAVAGE FEEDING

### Preparation

- If the feeding is to be given by gravity, an IV pole may be used. If the feeding is to be given by pump, gather the necessary bag and tubing. Prime the appropriate tubing, keeping the distal end covered.
- If possible, place the child in a semi-Fowler's position. If not, a prone or side-lying position is preferred to the supine position to decrease the risk of aspiration.

### Selected Equipment

Formula at room temperature (to prevent cramping)
Water for irrigation of the tube
Stethoscope
20-mL syringe to check tube placement

## Procedure—*Clean Gloves*

- Check the placement of the tube before each feeding by aspirating the stomach contents or auscultating over the abdomen while a small amount of air (5 mL or 10 mL in older children) is injected through the tube into the stomach.
- Assess the child's respiratory status and color. Changes in either may indicate that the nasogastric or orogastric tube is located in the trachea instead of in the esophagus.
- Once you are assured that the tube is in place, check gastric residuals and proceed with the steps necessary for the feeding.

## Bolus Feeding

- Aspirate the stomach contents to check the amount of residual. If the residual is less than half of the previous feeding, return the aspirated contents to the stomach. If the residual is greater, notify the physician.
- Attach the primed tubing from either the pump or the gravity set to the gastrostomy tube. Start the flow slowly while checking the patency of the tube. Set the rate and volume according to the physician's orders.
- When the feeding has been completed, assess the child's condition. Clamp and disconnect the tubing. Flush the tubing with a small amount of water to clean it.

## Continuous Feeding

- The procedure for continuous feeding is very similar to that for bolus feeding. However, the formula should hang no longer than 4 hours.
- When the feeding bag is hung, label it with the time and date.
- Change the feeding set once per shift or every 8 hours.
- Assess the child's condition and monitor respiratory status during the feeding.

## ▶ GASTRIC SUCTIONING

Both orogastric and nasogastric tubes can be connected to a suctioning device (Fig. 76) to provide either continuous or intermittent suction.

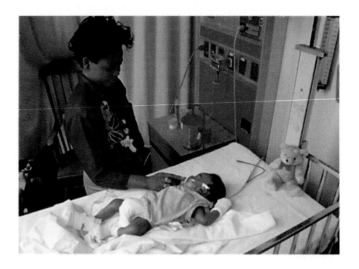

**FIGURE 76.** Nasogastric tube attached to a suctioning device.

## PERFORMING GASTRIC SUCTIONING

### Preparation

Before making the connection:
- Check the suction equipment.
- Check the tube for in proper position by aspirating the stomach contents or auscultating over the abdomen while a small amount of air (5 mL or 10 mL in older children) is injected through the tube into the stomach.
- Assess the child's respiratory status and color. Changes in either may indicate that the tube is located in the trachea instead of in the esophagus.

### Procedure—*Clean Gloves*

- Attach the suction to the orogastric or nasogastric tube at its distal end. Tape the connection site.
- Turn the suction to the setting ordered by the physician. Observe the color, amount, and character of the contents suctioned.
- Record the child's response (vital signs, complaints of abdominal discomfort).
- Monitor the child's condition frequently and label the level of the contents collected.

# ELIMINATION 11

## ► URINARY CATHETERIZATION

Urinary catheterization is performed to obtain sterile urine for diagnostic purposes, to measure the amount of urine in the bladder accurately, to empty the bladder, or to relieve bladder distention. In the hospital setting, urinary catheterization is performed as a sterile procedure using sterile gloves. Additional protective wear such as a gown and goggles should be used if the child is resistant or if splashing of urine is possible. For children outside the hospital who require intermittent catheterization to maintain an empty bladder, it is done as a sterile or clean procedure. (Refer to Table 16–6 in Ball and Bindler's *Pediatric Nursing* for a description of home care teaching for clean intermittent catheterization.)

## PERFORMING A URINARY CATHETERIZATION

### RECOMMENDED URINARY CATHETER SIZES

- Infant: 4–5 French
- Toddler and preschooler: 6 French
- School-age child: 6–10 French
- Adolescent: 8–12 French

### Preparation

- Check the physician's orders to determine whether intermittent or indwelling catheterization is planned. Determine the size of the catheter based on the child's size, age, and weight. Sizes vary from 4 to 12 French. A feeding tube may be used for an infant requiring intermittent catheterization.
- The child needs to be held in position for the catheterization procedure. If the parents wish to stay in the room with the child, encourage them to stand at the head of the bed and hold the child's hand.

### Selected Equipment

Sterile urinary catheterization tray (containing sterile gloves, drapes, antiseptic solution, cotton swabs or balls, forceps, lubricant, and container for urine)

Correct type and size of catheter (nonlatex if the child has a latex allergy or sensitivity or is catheterized often)

A container to receive soiled cotton balls

If an indwelling catheter is to be inserted, a syringe filled with normal saline is needed to inflate the balloon. The amount required is noted on the balloon port. Tape and a drainage collection apparatus are also needed.

### Procedure—*Sterile Gloves*

- Place clean pads under the child's perineum.
- Open the tray, maintaining the sterile field. Open the lubricant and squeeze it onto the sterile field. Pour the antiseptic over the cotton swabs or balls.
- Put on the sterile gloves. Lubricate the tip of the catheter and place the distal end in the tray.
- Have an assistant position and restrain the child.

### *Female*

- Clean the perineum. With your nondominant hand, spread the labia apart. With your dominant (sterile) hand, pick up the antiseptic-saturated cotton balls with the forceps. Clean the meatus, using one ball for each wipe, in a front-to-back motion along each side of the labia minora, along the sides of the urinary meatus, and finally straight down over the urethral opening. Discard each cotton ball away from the sterile field.
- Pick up the lubricated catheter tip with your dominant hand, keeping the distal end in the container. Gently insert the tip into the meatus (approximately 2.5 cm [1 in.] in the child) until there is a free flow of urine. If resistance is felt, do not force the catheter. You may try again with another sterile catheter, preferably one size smaller.
- Once the catheter is in place, collect the urine specimen while holding the catheter with your nondominant hand.

### Male

- Clean the perineum. With your nondominant hand, hold the penis behind the glans and spread the meatus with your thumb and forefinger. Retract the foreskin if the child is uncircumcised. With your dominant (sterile) hand, pick up the antiseptic-saturated cotton balls with the forceps. Clean the tissue surrounding the meatus using one cotton ball for each wipe in an outward circular fashion. Discard each cotton ball away from the sterile field.
- Pick up the lubricated catheter tip with your dominant hand, keeping the distal end in the container. Lift the penis, exerting slight traction until it is perpendicular with the body. Insert the catheter steadily into the meatus until there is a free flow of urine. Have the child blow out to relax the peritoneal muscles. If resistance is felt, do not force the catheter. You may try to insert another sterile catheter, preferably one size smaller.
- Once the catheter is in place, lower the penis and collect the urine specimen while holding the catheter with your nondominant hand.

### For a Laboratory Specimen

- To obtain urine for laboratory analysis, follow the preceding sequence each time urine is to be obtained.
- Drain the bladder of urine.
- Remove the catheter after the specimen has been collected.
- Cap the specimen, label, and send to the lab.

### For Indwelling Catheter

- Attach tubing to the drainage apparatus.
- Tape tubing to the leg to avoid pulling.
- Inflate balloon on catheter to recommended amount.
- Be sure tubing has no kinks and does not drop below bladder level at any point.
- Hang drainage apparatus on the bed frame. Aviod bed rails to prevent pulling on catheter.

# ► OSTOMY CARE

Ostomies are performed when an infant or child requires fecal or urinary diversion. Infants and children may require an ostomy for several reasons, including necrotizing enterocolitis, Hirschsprung's disease, imperforate anus, prune-belly syndrome, inflammatory bowel syndrome, spina bifida, tumor, and trauma. An ileostomy, colostomy, or urinary diversion is performed depending on the disorder and its location.

An adhesive appliance is usually applied just after surgery to measure drainage. If a dressing is applied instead of an adhesive appliance, the drainage can be measured by weighing the dressing both before and after saturation. For each 1-g increase in weight of the dressing, approximately 1 mL of fluid has drained into it.

In children and infants, ostomies pose special problems because of the fragility of the skin. Care must be taken to prevent skin breakdown at the site.

## CHANGING THE DRESSING FOR AN INFANT WITH AN OSTOMY

### Procedure—*Clean Gloves*

- After each bowel movement, change the dressing, clean and dry the skin, and apply a nonporous substance.
- To absorb drainage, place gauze with slits cut to fit around the stoma. Use tape to hold the gauze in place. Alternatively, Montgomery straps, an Ace wrap, or a diaper can be used to protect the skin.

*Note:* Once the stoma has healed and the infant is large enough to wear a pouch, an appliance with a Stomahesive wafer will be used.

## CHANGING AN OSTOMY POUCH FOR AN INFANT OR CHILD

**Procedure**—*Clean Gloves*

- Empty the pouch when it is one third to one half full. Remove the pouch, and place it in a sealable plastic bag for disposal.
- Children will commonly have Stomahesive around the stoma. This is a wafer of protective material to which a pouch can be attached or removed, thus protecting the integrity of the skin. Most wafers need to be changed only once a week.
- Wash the skin and the stoma gently. Note any skin breakdown or signs of infection. Dry the area. Check the condition of the Stomahesive.
- Prepare the new pouch. Place it on the Stomahesive. Press the pouch firmly against the Stomahesive to form a tight seal. Be careful to avoid making any wrinkles. Close the opening of the pouch with the appropriate clamp.

## ► ENEMAS

There are three important considerations when giving an enema to an infant or a child: the type of fluid, the amount of fluid, and the appropriate distance to insert the tube into the rectum (Table 9).

Generally, an isotonic fluid such as normal saline is used for children. However, a commercial hypertonic product, such as a pediatric Fleet enema is sometimes used.

| 9 Considerations in Administering an Enema | | |
| --- | --- | --- |
| Age | Volume (mL) | Distance to Be Inserted (cm) [in.] |
| Infant | 40–100 | 2.5 [1] |
| Toddler | 100–200 | 5.0 [2] |
| Preschooler | 200–300 | 5.0 [2] |
| School-age child | 300–500 | 7.5 [3] |
| Adolescent | 500–700 | 10.0 [4] |

## ADMINISTERING AN ENEMA

### Preparation

Assure the child that a bedpan will be kept at the bedside. If the child is toilet trained, be sure to place him or her in a bed near a bathroom before giving the enema.

### Selected Equipment

Ordered solution (in container with attached tip) *or* enema bag and rectal tube (size 14–18 French for child; 12 French for infant)
Solution container
Ordered fluid
Water-soluble lubricant

### Procedure—*Clean Gloves, Gown*

- Place absorbent pads on the bed. Position the child on his or her left side, with the knees drawn up to the chest or right leg flexed over the left leg. You may need an assistant to hold the child in position.
- If a rectal tube is being used, attach the solution container, add the fluid, and purge the tubing and tube. Lubricate the tip. If a Fleet enema is being used, the tip is prelubricated.

- Gently insert the tip to the recommended distance. Allow the fluid to run in slowly, for at least 10 to 15 minutes. If the child complains of cramping, stop the infusion to allow the child to rest, then continue.
- Infants and children may not be able to retain the fluid. Holding the buttocks together might help.
- When the child is ready or when it is time to expel the contents of the enema, place the bedpan on the bed or escort the child to the bathroom. Provide privacy as requested. Assess for dizziness or weakness before leaving.
- Clean the perineum. The child or parent may choose to perform this step.
- Help the child resume a position of comfort.
- Assess the return for amount and character.

# IRRIGATION 12

► UNIT OUTLINE

**EAR IRRIGATION**
*Performing an ear irrigation*

**EYE IRRIGATION**
*Performing an eye irrigation*

## ► EAR IRRIGATION

**NURSING ALERT**

Ear irrigation should not be performed if there is any drainage from the child's ear. The tympanic membrane may not be intact.

Irrigation of the ear is performed to remove cerumen or a foreign body. Frequently the child has symptoms of otitis media but the canal cannot be visualized. Always ask the parent if there has been any drainage from the ear and examine the ear with an otoscope (see Chapter 3 of Ball and Bindler's *Pediatric Nursing* for a description of proper use of the otoscope and normal ear landmarks). If there is drainage, contact the physician before irrigating the ear. Be sure to reexamine with the otoscope after about 1 minute of irrigation to observe the effects of treatment.

## PERFORMING AN EAR IRRIGATION

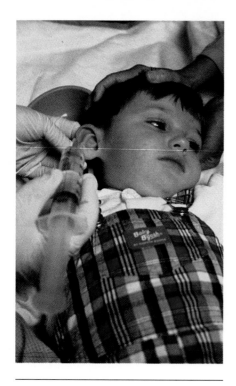

FIGURE 77. Ear irrigation.

### Selected Equipment

Ordered solution, warmed to room temperature
Irrigating syringe (bulb or Asepto) with tubing or Water Pik

### Procedure—*Clean Gloves*

- Check the physician's orders for the type of fluid to be administered.
- Examine the ear with an otoscope.
- Position the child on his or her back. For the child less than 3 years of age, gently pull the pinna straight back and slightly downward to straighten the ear canal. For the older child, pull the pinna back and upward.
- Place an emesis basin under the ear to be irrigated. Place a waterproof pad on the bed under the head (Fig. 77).
- Draw 20 mL of warm ordered solution into a syringe with the tubing attached.
- Gently flush the solution into the ear canal, catching the draining fluid with the emesis basin.
- Alternately, use a Water Pik at the lowest setting to flush the ear.
- Repeat according to prescriber's orders.
- Reexamine the ear with an otoscope and record changes from the treatment.
- Dry the child's ear, cheek, and neck.

## ► EYE IRRIGATION

Irrigation of the eye is performed to flush out a foreign body or a chemical irritant (Fig. 78). Children often close the injured eye tightly, so getting them to relax for this procedure is important. Care must be taken not to touch the cornea, which could cause further eye injury. Careful aseptic technique is needed to prevent infection.

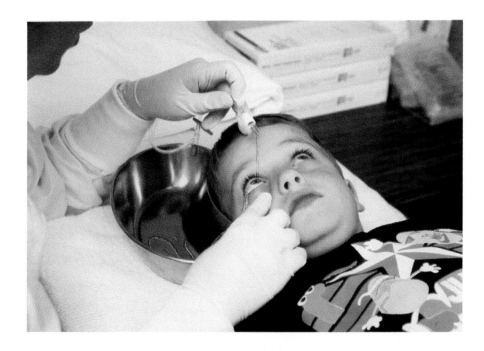

FIGURE 78. Eye irrigation.

## PERFORMING AN EYE IRRIGATION

### Preparation

- Check the physician's orders for the volume and type of fluid to be used (most often sterile normal saline).
- The child will need to be held in position for this procedure. An assistant can hold the child supine with his or her body over the child's, keeping the child's head turned slightly so that the eye to be irrigated is lower than the other eye. This method is used to avoid cross-contamination of the eye not being irrigated.
- Attach the IV tubing to the bag of room temperature normal saline. Purge the line, but keep the tip covered.

### Procedure—*Sterile Gloves*

- Place absorbent pads under the child's head, neck, and shoulders, using towels for extra absorption. Place an emesis basin under the lower eye to catch drainage.
- Using the thumb and forefinger of your dominant hand, gently separate the child's lids.
- Remove the cover from the IV tubing. Open the clamp midway, pointing the stream of fluid into the lower conjunctival sac from the inner to the outer canthus. Periodically turn off the stream of solution and have the child close the eye so that the solution can also move into the upper conjunctival area.
- When the irrigation has been completed, dry the child's eye gently with gauze or a cotton ball from the inner to the outer canthus.
- Assess the return for color, odor, and character.

# APPENDICES

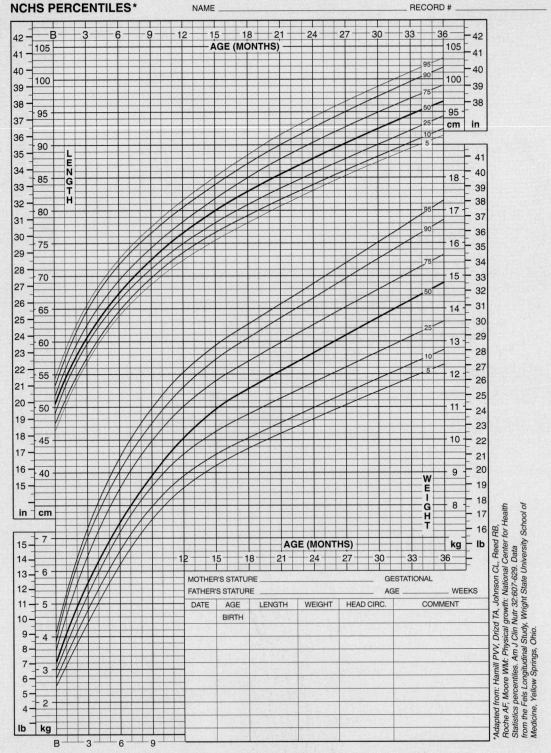

**BOYS: BIRTH TO 36 MONTHS**
**PHYSICAL GROWTH**
**NCHS PERCENTILES***

NAME _____ RECORD # _____

**FIGURE A–1.** Physical growth percentiles for length and weight—boys: birth to 36 months.

# Physical Growth Charts

**BOYS: BIRTH TO 36 MONTHS**
**PHYSICAL GROWTH**
**NCHS PERCENTILES***     NAME _____     RECORD # _____

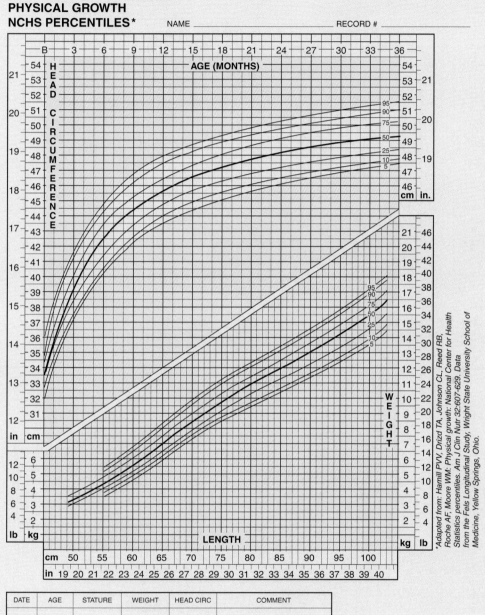

Reprinted with permission
of Ross Laboratories

*Adapted from: Hamill PVV, Drizd TA, Johnson CL, Reed RB, Roche AF, Moore WM: Physical growth: National Center for Health Statistics percentiles. Am J Clin Nutr 32:607-629. Data from the Fels Longitudinal Study, Wright State University School of Medicine, Yellow Springs, Ohio.

**FIGURE A–2.** Physical growth percentiles for head circumference, length, and weight—boys: birth to 36 months.
*From NCHS Growth Charts, copyright © 1982 Ross Laboratories. Reprinted with permission of Ross Laboratories, Columbus OH 43216.*

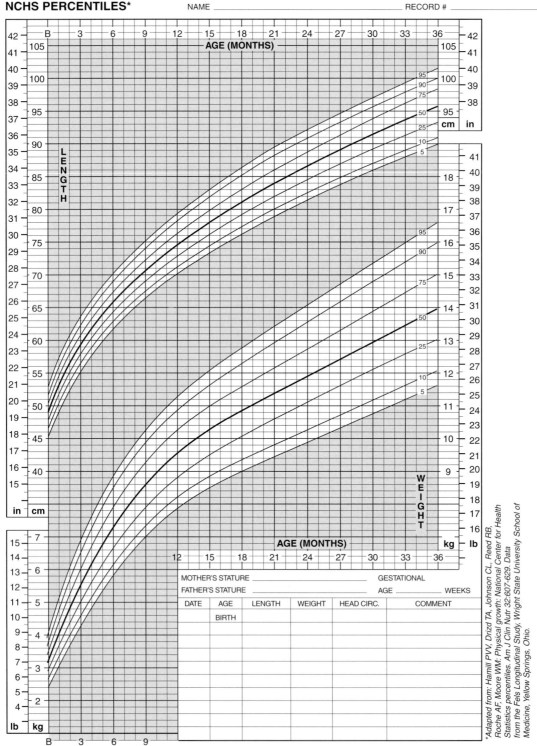

**FIGURE A–3.** Physical growth percentiles for length and weight—girls: birth to 36 months.
*From NCHS Growth Charts, copyright © 1982 Ross Laboratories. Reprinted with permission of Ross Laboratories, Columbus OH 43216.*

## GIRLS: BIRTH TO 36 MONTHS
## PHYSICAL GROWTH
## NCHS PERCENTILES*

NAME _____  RECORD # _____

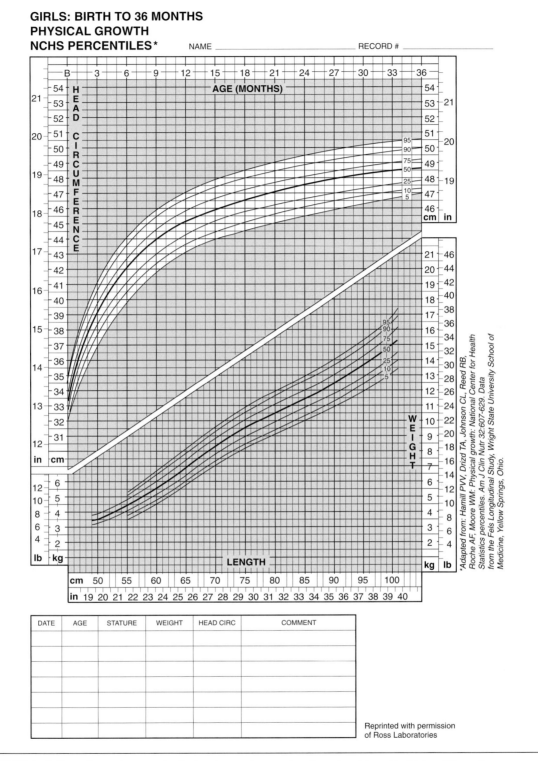

Reprinted with permission
of Ross Laboratories

**FIGURE A–4.** Physical growth percentiles for head circumference, length, and weight—girls: birth to 36 months.
*From NCHS Growth Charts, copyright © 1982 Ross Laboratories. Reprinted with permission of Ross Laboratories, Columbus OH 43216.*

**BOYS: 2 TO 18 YEARS**
**PHYSICAL GROWTH**
**NCHS PERCENTILES***

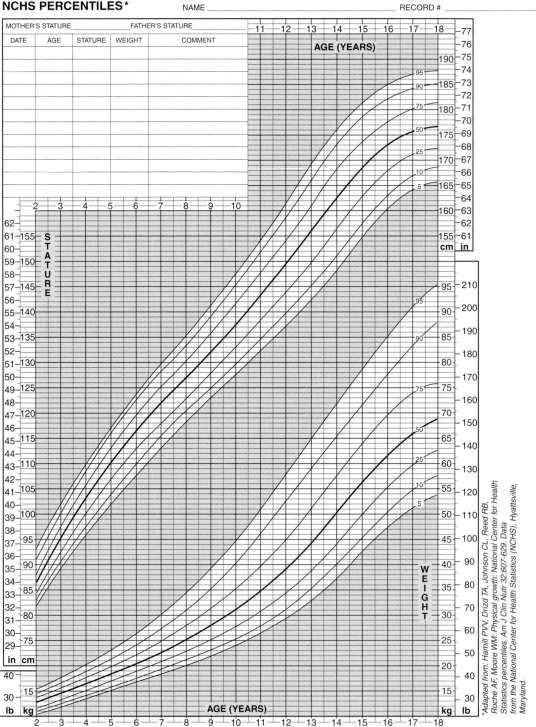

**FIGURE A–5.** Physical growth percentiles for stature and weight according to age—boys: 2 to 18 years.
*From NCHS Growth Charts, copyright © 1982 Ross Laboratories. Reprinted with permission of Ross Laboratories, Columbus OH 43216.*

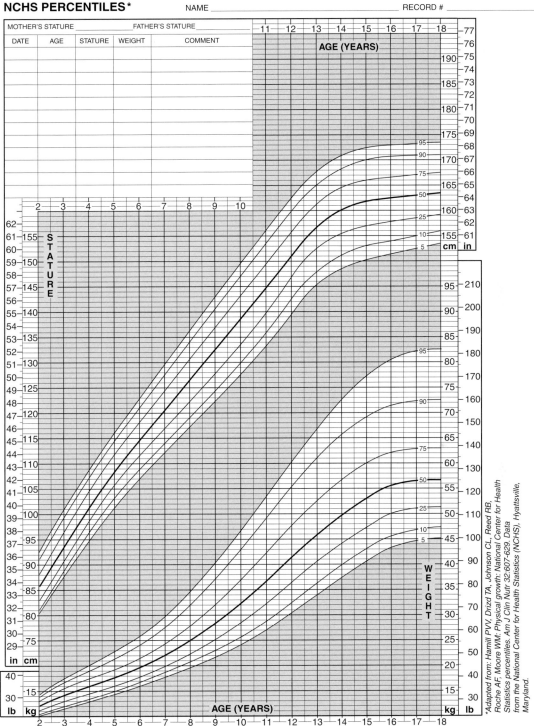

**GIRLS: 2 TO 18 YEARS**
**PHYSICAL GROWTH**
**NCHS PERCENTILES***

**FIGURE A–6.** Physical growth percentiles for stature and weight according to age—girls: 2 to 18 years.
*From NCHS Growth Charts, copyright © 1982 Ross Laboratories. Reprinted with permission of Ross Laboratories, Columbus OH 43216.*

## FAMILY STRUCTURE

- Do you want to care for your child at home?
- Are you aware of any alternatives to home care?
- Who are your child's primary caregivers?
- Who are the other members of your household?
- Can you identify another person to act as backup caregiver for your child?
- Are there others (friends/family members) who can assist you with your child with special needs, with your other children, or with your family obligations?

## MEDICAL MANAGEMENT

- Have you completed the hospital training in your child's care? If no, what is left to learn?
- Has your child's backup caregiver completed training? If no, what is left to learn?
- Do you or your backup caregiver need refresher training for anything?
- Do you have transportation to medical appointments?
- Do you need help in selecting a nursing provider?
- Do you need help in selecting a vendor?

## NUTRITION

- How is your child fed?
- If formula, will you need help to buy/locate the formula?
- Have you applied for WIC?
- Does your child have a special need for diapers that is greater than the norm?

## EDUCATION

- Will your child be going out to school?
- Do you know which school your child will attend?
- Has your child been referred for the Infant and Toddler program?
- Do you have an IFSP for your child? An IEP?
- Do you have a contact person in the school program?
- Will your child need adaptive equipment at home?

## PARENTING/CHILD CARE

- During what hours/shifts do you think you will need nursing for your child?
- In the event you need to leave home quickly or if you become incapacitated, who will watch your child with special needs? Who will watch your other children?

Key: WIL = Women, Infant, Children Nutrition Program; IFSP = Individualized Family Service Plan; IEP = Individualized Education Plan; TANF = Temporary Assistance for Needy Families

From McCord, B. (1993). *Family Profile*. Millersville, MD: Coordinating Center for Home and Community Care.

- What is your plan for child care in the event of the nurse's absence?
- Will you need help in finding day care for your other children?
- Do you work outside the home? Any plans for the future?
- Do you go to school? Any plans for the future?

## FINANCIAL RESOURCES

- Does your child have medical insurance? Are your other children covered under a family insurance plan?
- Do you need more information about or referrals to WIC, SSI, TANF, Food Stamps, Housing, Respite Care?
- Do you need help in obtaining everyday supplies for your child?
- Do you need a referral for help in obtaining other items for your child, such as furniture, clothing, toys?
- Do you need help with budgeting?

## COMMUNITY RESOURCES

- Are you involved with any other helping agencies or persons, especially those you would like to include in this planning process?

- Do you or other family members belong to a church? Social groups? Clubs? Associations?
- Would you like to talk to another parent who has a child with special needs?
- Would you like a referral to a support group?
- Do you want a referral for counseling? Individual? Marital? Family? Child? Sibling?

## FAMILY LIFE

- Do you see your child's homecoming as making a significant change in your lifestyle, and if so, how?
- Do you have concerns about your other children?
- Can you describe how you see your child in a few months? What are your short-term goals for your child?
- Can you describe how you see your child in a few years? What are your long-term goals for your child?
- How would you describe your family strengths?
- What are your family's needs at this time?

Vaccines[a] are listed under the routinely recommended ages. [Bars] indicate range of acceptable ages for vaccination. (Shaded ovals) indicate *catch-up vaccination*: at 11–12 years of age, hepatitis B vaccine should be administered to children not previously vaccinated, and varicella vaccine should be administered to children not previously vaccinated who lack a reliable history of chickenpox.

| Age ▶ / Vaccine ▼ | Birth | 1 mo | 2 mo | 4 mo | 6 mo | 12 mo | 15 mo | 18 mo | 4–6 yr | 11–12 yr | 14–16 yr |
|---|---|---|---|---|---|---|---|---|---|---|---|
| Hepatitis B[b,c] | Hep B-1 | Hep B-1 | | | | | | | | | |
| | | Hep B-2 | Hep B-2 | Hep B-2 | Hep B-3 | Hep B-3 | Hep B-3 | Hep B-3 | | Hep B[c] | |
| Diphtheria, tetanus, pertussis[d] | | | DTaP or DTP | DTaP or DTP | DTaP or DTP | | DTaP or DTP[d] | DTaP or DTP[d] | DTaP or DTP | Td | Td |
| H. influenzae type b[e] | | | Hib | Hib | Hib[e] | Hib[e] | Hib[e] | | | | |
| Polio[f] | | | Polio[f] | Polio | Polio[f] | Polio[f] | Polio[f] | Polio[f] | Polio | | |
| Measles, mumps, rubella[g] | | | | | | MMR | MMR | | MMR[g] | MMR[g] | |
| Varicella[h] | | | | | | Var | Var | Var | | Var[h] | |

[a]This schedule indicates the recommended age for routine administration of currently licensed childhood vaccines. Some combination vaccines are available and may be used whenever administration of all components of the vaccine is indicated. Providers should consult the manufacturers' package inserts for detailed recommendations.

[b]*Infants born to HBsAg-negative mothers* should receive 2.5 μg of Merck vaccine (Recombivax HB) or 10 μg of SmithKline Beecham (SB) vaccine (Engerix-B). The 2nd dose should be administered ≥ 1 mo after the 1st dose. The 3rd dose should be given at least 2 months after the 2nd dose, but not before 6 mo of age.

*Infants born to HBsAg-positive mothers* should receive 0.5 mL hepatitis B immune globulin (HBIG) within 12 hr of birth, and either 5 μg of Merck vaccine (Recombivax HB) or 10 μg of SB vaccine (Engerix-B) at a separate site. The 2nd dose is recommended at 1–2 mo of age and the 3rd dose at 6 months of age.

*Infants born to mothers whose HBsAg status is unknown* should receive either 5 μg of Merck vaccine (Recombivax HB) or 10 μg of SB vaccine (Engerix-B) within 12 hr of birth. The 2nd dose of vaccine is recommended at 1 mo of age and the 3rd dose at 6 mo of age. Blood should be drawn at the time of delivery to determine the mother's HBsAg status; if it is positive, the infant should receive HBIG as soon as possible (no later than 1 wk of age). The dosage and timing of subsequent vaccine doses should be based upon the mother's HBsAg status.

[c]Children and adolescents who have not been vaccinated against hepatitis B in infancy may begin the series during any childhood visit. Those who have not previously received 3 doses of hepatitis B vaccine should initiate or complete the series during the 11–12-year-old visit and unvaccinated older adolescents should be vaccinated whenever possible. The 2nd dose should be administered at least 1 mo after the 1st dose, and the 3rd dose should be administered at least 4 mo after the 1st dose and at least 2 mo after the 2nd dose.

[d]DTaP (diphtheria and tetanus toxoids and acellular pertussis vaccine) is the preferred vaccine for all doses in the vaccination series, including completion of the series in children who have received ≥ 1 dose of whole-cell DTP vaccine. Whole-cell DTP is an acceptable alternative to DTaP. The 4th dose of DTaP may be administered as early as 12 mo of age, provided 6 mo have elapsed since the 3rd dose, and if the child is considered unlikely to return at 15–18 mo of age. Td (tetanus and diphtheria toxoids, absorbed, for adult use) is recommended at 11–12 yr of age if at least 5 yr have elapsed since the last dose of DTP, DTaP, or DT. Subsequent routine Td boosters are recommended every 10 years.

[e]Three *H. influenzae* type b (Hib) conjugative vaccines are licensed for infant use. If PRP-OMP (PedvaxHIB [Merck]) is administered at 2 and 4 mo of age, a dose at 6 mo is not required. After completing the primary series, any Hib conjugate vaccine may be used as a booster.

[f]Two poliovirus vaccines are currently licensed in the United States: inactivated poliovirus vaccine (IPV) and oral poliovirus vaccine (OPV). The following schedules are all acceptable by the ACIP, the AAP, and the AAFP, and parents and providers may choose among them:
1. IPV at 2 and 4 mo; OPV at 12–18 mo and 4–6 yr
2. IPV at 2, 4, 12–18 mo, and 4–6 yr
3. OPV at 2, 4, 6–18 mo, and 4–6 yr

The ACIP routinely recommends schedule 1. IPV is the only poliovirus vaccine recommended for immunocompromised persons and their household contacts.

[g]The 2nd dose of MMR is routinely recommended at 4–6 yr of age or at 11–12 yr of age, but may be administered during any visit, provided at least 1 mo has elapsed since receipt of the 1st dose and that both doses are administered at or after 12 mo of age.

[h]Susceptible children may receive varicella vaccine (Var) at any visit after the first birthday, and those who lack a reliable history of chickenpox should be immunized during the 11–12-year-old visit. Children ≥ 13 yr of age should receive 2 doses, at least 1 mo apart.

# Pediatric Immunization Schedule

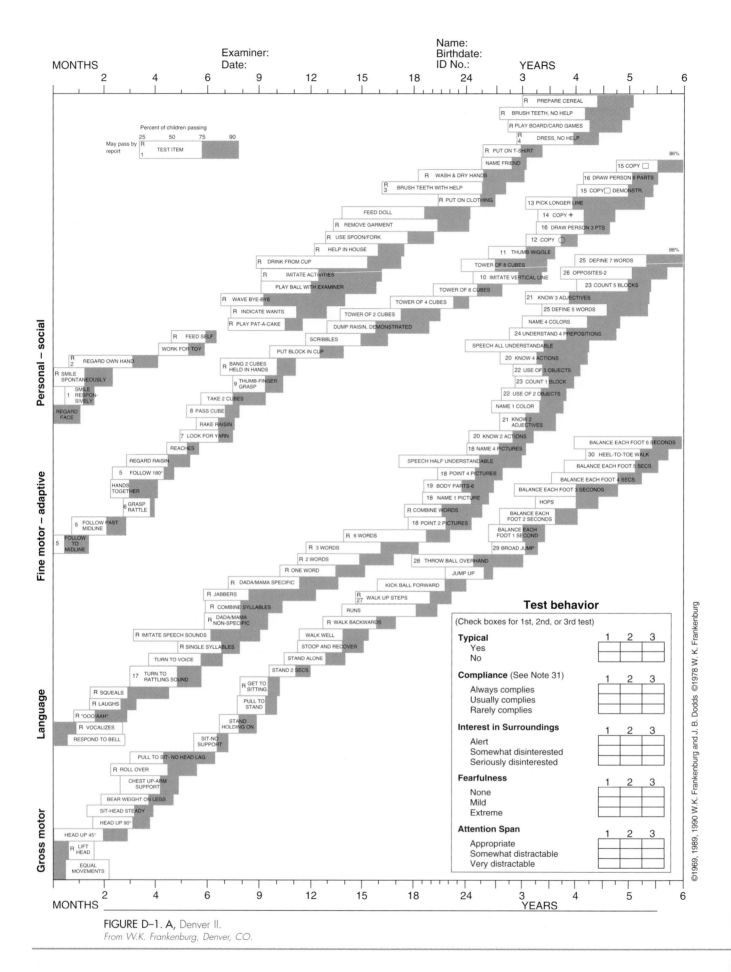

FIGURE D-1. A, Denver II.
*From W.K. Frankenburg, Denver, CO.*

## DIRECTIONS FOR ADMINISTRATION

1. Try to get child to smile by smiling, talking or waving. Do not touch him/her.
2. Child must stare at hand several seconds.
3. Parent may help guide toothbrush and put toothpaste on brush.
4. Child does not have to be able to tie shoes or button/zip in the back.
5. Move yarn slowly in an arc from one side to the other, about 8" above child's face.
6. Pass if child grasps rattle when it is touched to the backs or tips of fingers.
7. Pass if child tries to see where yarn went. Yarn should be dropped quickly from sight from tester's hand without arm movement.
8. Child must transfer cube from hand to hand without help of body, mouth, or table.
9. Pass if child picks up raisin with any part of thumb and finger.
10. Line can vary only 30 degrees or less from tester's line.
11. Make a fist with thumb pointing upward and wiggle only the thumb. Pass if child imitates and does not move any fingers other than the thumb.

12. Pass any enclosed form. Fail continuous round motions.
13. Which line is longer? (Not bigger.) Turn paper upside down and repeat. (pass 3 of 3 or 5 of 6).
14. Pass any lines crossing near midpoint.
15. Have child copy first. If failed, demonstrate.

When giving items 12, 14, and 15, do not name the forms. Do not demonstrate 12 and 14.

16. When scoring, each pair (2 arms, 2 legs, etc.) counts as one part.
17. Place one cube in cup and shake gently near child's ear, but out of sight. Repeat for other ear.
18. Point to picture and have child name it. (No credit is given for sounds only.)
    If less than 4 pictures are named correctly, have child point to picture as each is named by tester.

19. Using doll, tell child: Show me the nose, eyes, ears, mouth, hands, feet, tummy, hair. Pass 6 of 8.
20. Using pictures, ask child: Which one flies?... says meow?... talks?... barks?... gallops? Pass 2 of 5, 4 of 5.
21. Ask child: What do you do when you are cold?... tired?... hungry? Pass 2 of 3, 3 of 3.
22. Ask child: What do you do with a cup? What is a chair used for? What is a pencil used for?
    Action words must be included in answers.
23. Pass if child correctly places <u>and</u> says how many blocks are on paper. (1, 5).
24. Tell child: Put block **on** table; **under** table; **in front of** me, **behind** me. Pass 4 of 4.
    (Do not help child by pointing, moving head or eyes.)
25. Ask child: What is a ball?... lake?... desk?... house?... banana?... curtain?... fence?... ceiling? Pass if defined in terms of use, shape, what it is made of, or general category (such as banana is fruit, not just yellow). Pass 5 of 8, 7 of 8.
26. Ask child: If a horse is big, a mouse is_____? If fire is hot, ice is_____? If sun shines during the day, the moon shines during the ____? Pass 2 of 3.
27. Child may use wall or rail only, not person. May not crawl.
28. Child must throw ball overhand 3 feet to within arm's reach of tester.
29. Child must perform standing broad jump over width of test sheet (8 1/2 inches).
30. Tell child to walk forward, ⊂⊃⊂⊃⊂⊃ → heel within 1 inch of toe. Tester may demonstrate.
    Child must walk 4 consecutive steps.
31. In the second year, half of normal children are non-compliant.

**OBSERVATIONS:**

FIGURE D–1. cont. B, Directions for administration of Denver II.
*From W.K. Frankenburg, Denver, CO.*

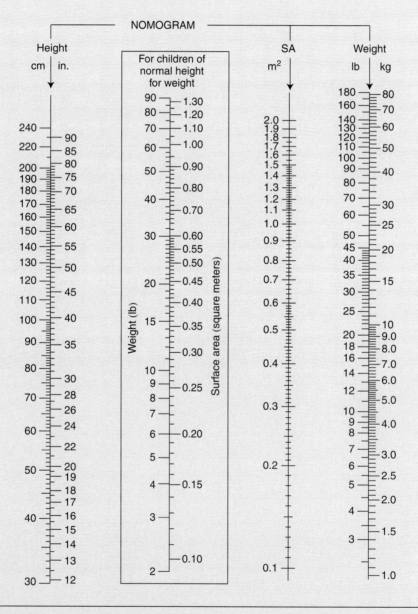

West nomogram for calculation of body surface area.
*Nomogram modified from data of E. Boyd by C.D. West; from Behrman, R.E., Kliegman, R.M., & Arvin, A.M. (Eds.) (1996). Nelson's textbook of pediatrics (15th ed.). Philadelphia: W.B. Saunders, p. 2079.*

# West Nomogram for Calculation of Body Surface Area

**EXAMPLE**

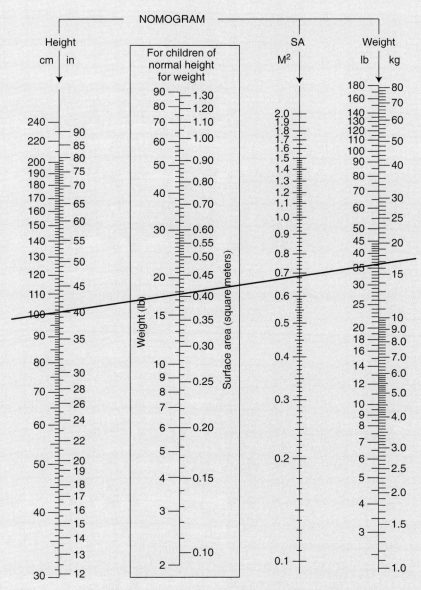

Pediatric doses of medications are generally based on body surface area (BSA) or weight. To calculate a child's BSA, draw a straight line from the height (in the left-hand column) to the weight (in the right-hand column). The point at which the line intersects the surface area (SA) column is the BSA (measured in square meters [$m^2$]). If the child is of roughly normal proportion, BSA can be calculated from the weight alone (in the enclosed area).

The following formula can then be used to estimate the pediatric drug dose:

$$\frac{\text{BSA of child}}{\text{Mean BSA of adult}} \times \text{Adult dose} = \text{Estimated pediatric dose}$$

## PATTERN 1: EXCHANGING

Altered Nutrition: More than Body Requirements
Altered Nutrition: Less than Body Requirements
Altered Nutrition: Risk for More than Body
   Requirements
Risk for Infection
Risk for Altered Body Temperature
Hypothermia
Hyperthermia
Ineffective Thermoregulation
Dysreflexia
Constipation
Perceived Constipation
Colonic Constipation
Diarrhea
Bowel Incontinence
Altered Urinary Elimination
Stress Incontinence
Reflex Incontinence
Urge Incontinence
Functional Incontinence
Total Incontinence
Urinary Retention
Altered (Specify Type) Tissue Perfusion (Renal,
   cerebral, cardiopulmonary, gastrointestinal,
   peripheral)
Fluid Volume Excess
Fluid Volume Deficit
Risk for Fluid Volume Deficit
Decreased Cardiac Output
Impaired Gas Exchange
Ineffective Airway Clearance
Ineffective Breathing Pattern
Inability to Sustain Spontaneous Ventilation
Dysfunctional Ventilatory Weaning Response
   (DVWR)
Risk for Injury
Risk for Suffocation
Risk for Poisoning
Risk for Trauma
Risk for Aspiration
Risk for Disuse Syndrome

Altered Protection
Impaired Tissue Integrity
Altered Oral Mucous Membrane
Impaired Skin Integrity
Risk for Impaired Skin Integrity
Decreased Adaptive Capacity: Intracranial
Energy Field Disturbance

## PATTERN 2: COMMUNICATING

Impaired Verbal Communication

## PATTERN 3: RELATING

Impaired Social Interaction
Social Isolation
Risk for Loneliness
Altered Role Performance
Altered Parenting
Risk for Altered Parent/Infant/Child Attachment
Sexual Dysfunction
Altered Family Processes
Caregiver Role Strain
Risk for Caregiver Role Strain
Altered Family Process: Alcoholism
Parental Role Conflict
Altered Sexuality Patterns

## PATTERN 4: VALUING

Spiritual Distress (Distress of the Human Spirit)
Potential for Enhanced Spiritual Well-Being

## PATTERN 5: CHOOSING

Ineffective Individual Coping
Impaired Adjustment
Defensive Coping
Ineffective Denial
Ineffective Family Coping: Disabling
Ineffective Family Coping: Compromised
Family Coping: Potential for Growth

# Approved Nursing Diagnoses— North American Nursing Diagnosis Association

Potential for Enhanced Community Coping
Ineffective Community Coping
Ineffective Management of Therapeutic Regimen (Individuals)
Noncompliance (Specify)
Ineffective Management of Therapeutic Regimen: Families
Ineffective Management of Therapeutic Regimen: Community
Effective Management of Therapeutic Regimen: Individual
Decisional Conflict (Specify)
Health-Seeking Behaviors (Specify)

## PATTERN 6: MOVING

Impaired Physical Mobility
Risk for Peripheral Neurovascular Dysfunction
Risk for Perioperative Positioning Injury
Activity Intolerance
Fatigue
Risk for Activity Intolerance
Sleep Pattern Disturbance
Diversional Activity Deficit
Impaired Home Maintenance Management
Altered Health Maintenance
Feeding Self-Care Deficit
Impaired Swallowing
Ineffective Breast-feeding
Interrupted Breast-feeding
Effective Breast-feeding
Ineffective Infant Feeding Pattern
Bathing/Hygiene Self-Care Deficit
Dressing/Grooming Self-Care Deficit
Toileting Self-Care Deficit
Altered Growth and Development
Relocation Stress Syndrome
Risk for Disorganized Infant Behavior
Disorganized Infant Behavior
Potential for Enhanced Organized Infant Behavior

## PATTERN 7: PERCEIVING

Body Image Disturbance
Self-Esteem Disturbance
Chronic Low Self-Esteem
Situational Low Self-Esteem
Personal Identity Disturbance
Sensory/Perceptual Alterations (Specify) (Visual, Auditory, Kinesthetic, Gustatory, Tactile, Olfactory)
Unilateral Neglect
Hopelessness
Powerlessness

## PATTERN 8: KNOWING

Knowledge Deficit (Specify)
Impaired Environmental Interpretation Syndrome
Acute Confusion
Chronic Confusion
Altered Thought Processes
Impaired Memory

## PATTERN 9: FEELING

Pain
Chronic Pain
Dysfunctional Grieving
Anticipatory Grieving
Risk for Violence: Self-Directed or Directed at Others
Risk for Self-Mutilation
Post-Trauma Response
Rape-Trauma Syndrome
Rape-Trauma Syndrome: Compound Reaction
Rape-Trauma Syndrome: Silent Reaction
Anxiety
Fear

American Heart Association. (1994). *Pediatric basic life support.* Dallas: Author.

———. (1992). Guidelines for cardiopulmonary resuscitation and emergency cardiac care. *Journal of the American Medical Association, 268*(16), 2251–2274.

Axton, S.E., Smith, L.F., Bertrand, S. Dhe, E., & Liehr, P. (1995). Comparison of brachial and calf blood pressures in infants. *Pediatric Nursing, 21*(4), 323–326.

Bindler, R.M., & Howry, L.B. (1997). *Pediatric drugs and nursing implications* (2nd ed.). Stamford, CT: Appleton & Lange.

Borton, D. (1997). Isolation precautions. *Nursing 97, 27*(1), 49–51.

Brown, S.L., Morrison, A.E., Parmentier, C.M., Woo, E.K., & Vishnwajjala, R.L. (1997). Infusions pump adverse events: Experience from medical service reports. *Journal of Intravenous Nursing, 20*(1), 41–49.

Camp, D., & Otten, N. (1990). How to insert and remove nasogastric tubes quickly and easily. *Nursing '90, 20*(9), 59–64.

Carroll, P. (1997). Pulse oximetry at your fingertips. *RN, 60*(2), 22–26.

———. (1995). CDC issues new infection control guidelines. *Journal of Intravenous Nursing, 18*(4), 207–209.

Chameides, L. (Ed.). (1994). *Textbook of pediatric advanced life support (2nd ed.).* Dallas: American Heart Association.

Committee on Pediatric Emergency Medicine. (1997). The use of physical restraint for children and adolescents in the acute care setting. *Pediatrics, 99*(3), 497–498.

Eichelberger, M., Ball, J., Pratsch, G., & Clark, J. (1998). *Pediatric emergencies: A manual for prehospital care providers* (2nd ed.). Upper Saddle River, NJ: Prentice-Hall.

Frederick, V. (1991). Pediatric IV therapy: Soothing the patient. *RN, 54*(12), 43–48.

Frey, A.M. (1995). Pediatric peripherally inserted central catheter program report. *Journal of Intravenous Nursing, 18*(6), 280–291.

Garner, J.S. (1996). Guideline for isolation precautions in hospitals. Part I. Evolution of isolation procedures. *American Journal of Infection Control, 24,* 24–31.

Gleeson, R. (1995). Use of non-latex gloves for children with latex allergies. *Journal of Pediatric Nursing, 10*(1), 64–65.

Gray, M. (1996). Atraumatic urethral catheterization of children. *Pediatric Nursing, 22*(4), 306–310.

Haddock, B.J., Merrow, D.C., & Swanson, M.S. (1996). The falling grace of axillary temperatures. *Pediatric Nursing, 22*(2), 121–125.

Hanna, D. (1995). Guidelines for pulse oximetry use in pediatrics. *Journal of Pediatric Nursing, 10*(2), 124–126.

Heximer, B. (1996). Troubleshooting G-tubes. *RN, 59*(7), 22–25.

Holder, C. (1990). New and improved guide to IV therapy. *American Journal of Nursing, 90*(2), 43–47.

Hospital Infection Control Practices Advisory Committee. (1996). Guideline for isolation precautions on hospitals. Part II. Recommendation for isolation precautions in hospitals. *American Journal of Infection Control, 24,* 32–52.

Lau, C.E. (1996). Transparent and gauze dressings and their effect on infection rates of central venous catheters: A review of past and current literature. *Journal of Intravenous Nursing, 19*(5), 240–245.

Mathews, P.J. (1997). Ventilator-associated infections. *Nursing, 27*(3), 50–51.

McAfee, T., Garland, L.R., & McNabb, T.S. (1990). How to safely draw blood from a vascular access device. *Nursing '90, 20*(11), 42–43.

Miracle, V., & Allnutt, D. (1990). How to perform basic airway management. *Nursing '90, 20*(4), 55–60.

O'Brien, R. (1991). Starting intravenous lines in children. *Journal of Emergency Nursing, 17*(4), 225–231.

Querin, J., & Stahl, L. (1990). Twelve simple steps for successful blood transfusions. *Nursing '90, 20*(10), 79–81.

Reed, T., & Phillips, S. (1996). Management of central venous catheter occlusions and repairs. *Journal of Intravenous Nursing, 19*(6), 289–294.

Robatham, G., Woodger, S., & Merante, D. (1995). A prospective study evaluating the effects of extending total parenteral nutrition line changes to 72 hours. *Journal of Intravenous Nursing, 18*(2), 84–87.

Skale, N. (1992). *Manual of pediatric nursing procedures.* Philadelphia: J.B. Lippincott.

Smith, R.L., & Sheperd, M. (1995). Central venous catheter infection rates in an acute care hospital. *Journal of Intravenous Nursing, 18*(5), 255–262.

Smith, S., & Duell, D. (1996). *Clinical nursing skills* (4th ed.). Norwalk, CT: Appleton & Lange.

Speer, K.M., & Swann, C.L. (1993). *The Addison-Wesley manual of pediatric nursing procedures.* Menlo Park, CA: Addison-Wesley.

Swearingen, P. (Ed.). (1996). *Photo atlas of nursing procedures* (3rd ed.). Menlo Park, CA: Addison-Wesley.

Viall, C.D. (1990). Your complete guide to central venous catheters. *Nursing '90, 20*(2), 34–42.

Zimmerman, S., et al. (1991). *Orientation manual for the emergency medical trauma center, Children's National Medical Center.* Washington, DC: Unpublished.

# INDEX OF CLINICAL SKILLS

Page numbers followed by *t* and *f* indicate tables and figures, respectively.